INTUITION

and

EGO
STATES

Tony Lofting 1974

Headquarters of the
International Transactional Analysis Association
San Francisco

INTUITION

and

EGO STATES

THE ORIGINS OF TRANSACTIONAL ANALYSIS

A Series of Papers

By **ERIC BERNE, MD**

Edited by Paul McCormick

Published in San Francisco by

HARPER & ROW, PUBLISHERS

New York, Hagerstown, San Francisco, London

Printed in the United States of America
Design by R. C. Schuettge Book Productions
Typeset by Vera Allen Composition, Castro Valley, California

Library of Congress Cataloging in Publication Data

Berne, Eric.
    Intuition and ego states.

    Bibliography: p.
    Includes index.
    1. Intuition (Psychology)—Addresses, essays,
lectures. 2. Ego (Psychology)—Addresses, essays,
lectures. 3. Transactional analysis—Addresses,
essays, lectures. I. Title.
RC489.T7B465   616.8'914   76-57549
ISBN 06–060784–x

77 78 79 80 81 10 9 8 7 6 5 4 3 2 1

Contents

The International Transactional Analysis Association (ITAA)

THE INTERNATIONAL Transactional Analysis Association (1772 Vallejo St., San Francisco, CA 94123) is a nonprofit, educational corporation of more than 10,000 members, 1,500 of them from 41 countries other than the USA. Its purpose is to serve the membership, and others, in the application and development of transactional analysis (TA), originated by Eric Berne, MD.

In the late 1950s and throughout the 60s, Dr. Berne and his colleagues evolved TA as a comprehensive system for group and individual psychotherapy, for personal growth and behavior change, and for the improvement of human relations generally. The ITAA, founded in 1964 as an outgrowth of Dr. Berne's weekly San Francisco Social Psychiatry Seminars, includes clinicians in all of the psychotherapeutic and counseling arts, and professionals from many other fields, including business, education, religion, and health care.

Membership levels range from Regular (those who complete an introductory course) to Advanced, which includes Clinical and Special Fields (trained appliers of TA who have passed written and oral examinations). Teaching Membership, the highest level, authorizes a person to train and supervise advanced membership candidates.

An ITAA Directory designates all who have been certified as TA psychotherapists or special fields practitioners.

Editor's Preface

ERIC BERNE DOES MORE in these pages than penetrate the mysteries of intuition. He explains the fascinating course that leads him to found a whole psychotherapeutic system, transactional analysis (TA), that extraordinary aid in the fathoming of human affairs. These historically important articles describe, as only a primary source can, the evolution of Dr. Berne's insights and awarenesses, from those of an orthodox psychoanalyst to those of an originator of an almost defiantly new approach in psychotherapy.

He does not begin the series with any such description in mind, of course, but that is what it turns out to be.

The first paper, "The Nature of Intuition," is finished in 1949, a year in which he is still in his own analysis (with Erik Erikson), still aspiring to the official title *psychoanalyst*. When he publishes the last one, "The Psychodynamics of Intuition," in 1962, eight years have passed since he has started his first TA group, embryonic though it is. (Readers may see from that last article, and from all of Berne's books for that matter, that he has not disavowed his indebtedness to Freudian theory, regardless of his having parted from the Freudians.)

These eight papers trace the story, from his early experiments with intuition (for which he had an uncanny gift) to the evidence (by way of primal imagery, primal judgment, and ego imagery) that each of us is not just one personality but a combination of three, Parent, Adult, and Child, all residing in one skin. Here he briefly explains how this threesome complicates self-knowledge, communication, social behavior, and personal destinies, subjects he develops at greater length in *Transactional Analysis in Psychotherapy, Games People Play, What Do You Say After You Say Hello*, and other books.

But in this one he reveals the origins of TA, and they are deep-rooted.

All but the first article have been edited slightly (brackets and ellipsis points indicate where) to avoid repetition, but some overlapping has been left to show how the writings build on one another.

Here is an opportunity for readers, newcomers to TA or not, to learn much more about Eric Berne, intuition, the complexities of psychotherapy, the roots of TA, and themselves as well.

TA Press and the International Transactional Analysis Association acknowledge the generosity of the original publishers who have permitted the reissuance of the papers here: *The Psychiatric Quarterly, The American Journal of Psychotherapy*, and *The International Record of Medicine*.

Thanks from the editor go to the manager of Transactional Publications, Hank Maiden; to the president of the ITAA, William H. Holloway, MD; and to the ITAA executive director, Robert Andersen, for their direction and assistance in the preparation of this book.

Paul McCormick

1 The Nature of Intuition

UNDER FAVORABLE CONDITIONS most, if not all, human beings, particularly specialists in science and commerce, make judgments about everyday matters in their field by processes they cannot ordinarily explain. They form their judgments of reality, probably, by integrating a series of cognitive processes (cf. Bergson, 1944). For purposes of investigation, one can separate this possibly continuous series into artificial segments. Circumstances seem to determine which segment of the series contributes most to the verbalized perception.

First, judgments can be made by means of logic and actively directed, verbalized perception: e.g., the clinical diagnosis of schizophrenia as made by a group of medical students. This is a conscious process.

Second, they can be made by means of unverbalized processes and observations based on previously formulated knowledge which has become integrated with the personality through long usage, and therefore functions below the level of consciousness: very much as the act of tying a shoelace must be learned by consciously thought-out steps, but later is performed "automatically" because the kinesthetic image has become integrated with the personality to such an extent that the conscious awareness

1

of how it is done is no longer required. This may be called a "secondarily subconscious" process. (Cf. "repression proper" or "after-expulsion"—Freud.) The diagnosis of schizophrenia as made by a specialist may be based on such processes and sensory clues, which, having been verbalized at one time, are perceived and integrated at a later period below the threshold of consciousness (subconsciously*). He may make the diagnosis on sight and perhaps only later verbalize his mental processes for his students. The group of students makes the diagnosis by a conscious synthetic process, while the specialist may make it by an intuitive process which he is afterward able to analyze.

Third, judgments can be made with the help of clues whose formulation has not yet become or may never become conscious, but which nevertheless are based on sense impressions, including smell. (Cf. "primal repression"—Freud.) This may be called a "primary subconscious" process. The professional weight-guesser makes continual use of this intuitive process. His uncannily accurate guesses are based on sensory data which he cannot adequately analyze or verbalize, just as the painter may uncannily convey the age and vicissitudes of his subject through his nonverbal medium. The present study is chiefly concerned with this type of intuition, and the writer's observations show that such intuitions are synthesized from discrete sensory elements ("subliminal perceptions") whose perception and synthesis both take place below the threshold of consciousness. Analagous perceptions are spoken of by Freud as forming part of the "day's residue" in dreams.

---

*This is a legitimate use of a word many people prefer to avoid. Here it is comfortable since it includes both preconscious and unconscious.

Fourth, they may be made in ways which are quite unexplainable by what we know at present concerning sense perceptions.

The first method is evidently a function of the conscious perceptive system. The second and third methods are probably functions of preconscious systems, since they can be brought into conscious analysis relatively easily, and because of their analogy to the use of preconscious material in dreams. The indications are that the fourth method is a function of unconscious systems (cf. Eisenbud, 1946).

It is probable that judgments, about other people at any rate, are in most cases, if not all, a function of the whole epistemological series and rarely, if ever, the outcome of only one of these artificial segments of it. Since this discussion is mainly concerned with the third method, however, that which has been termed "primarily subconscious," it should be noted that various authors have expressed valuable opinions which can assist in differentiating the use of such processes in making judgments about people.

There is a class of "hunches" in everyday life and of judgments in clinical practice which appear to lack a specific basis in conscious or preconscious experience, and which probably belong here. Such are the experiences of "listening with the third ear" described by T. Reik (1948). Since we can throw little light on their mechanisms, they will be called simply "hunches." E.J. Kempf (1921, p. 23), somewhat like Darwin, speaks of understanding emotional states in others by "reflex imitation through similar brief muscle tensions," and states that by this token "in a certain sense we think with our muscles." This method of judgment may be called "intuition through subjective experience" (proprioception). A similar method can be useful clinically in interpreting handwriting, Bender Gestalt tests, and some material in Rorschach tests. This is a little different from the type of intuitive judgment which is based upon extensive clinical experience, such as has been cited in the case of weight-guessers and which will be enlarged upon here in later clinical material. In Jung's terminology, (1946, pp. 567-569) intuitions of the latter type are "objective" and "concrete." Such intuitions may be termed "intuition through objective experience."

Many authors have described other types of "intuition" under that name (Poincaré, 1948) or something similar, such as "inspiration," (Kris, 1939) "insight," (Hutchinson, 1939) etc. On the other hand, many of the magnificent edifices of the philosophers, such as Kant, Descartes, and Locke, use the concept of intuition as one of their building blocks. If we aspire here only to consider what is commonly called "clinical intuition," we avoid the dangers run by those who try to scale the walls of philosophy. The philosophical aspects have been discussed by K.W. Wild (1938).

For the present purpose it is only necessary to define intuition sufficiently to separate it from its nearest neighbors. A pragmatic definition, based on clinical experience, may be stated as follows:

Intuition is knowledge based on experience and acquired through sensory contact with the subject, without the "intuiter" being able to formulate to himself or others exactly how he came to his conclusions. Or in psychological terminology, it is knowledge based on experience and acquired by means of preverbal unconscious or preconscious functions through sensory contact with the subject. This approximates the definition of Jung (ibid.), who says that intuition "is that psychological function which transmits perceptions in an unconscious way." It is even something like the dictionary definition: "the quick perception of truth without conscious attention or reasoning." (Funk & Wagnalls.)

This concept of clinical intuition implies that the individual can know something without knowing how he knows it. ("That distant cow is sick.") If he can correctly formulate the grounds for his conclusions, we say that they are based on logical thought ("This cow is sick because . . . ") and actively directed observation ("This is obviously the sick one"). If his conclusion seems to be based on something other than direct or indirect sensory contact with the subject ("Somewhere a cow is sick"), then we cannot help but be reminded of what J. B. Rhine calls "extra-sensory perception" (1937).

After careful consideration, it will be found that an interesting corollary must be added to this definition. Not only is the individual unaware of how he knows something; he may not even know what it is that he knows, but behaves or reacts in a specific way as if *(als ob)* his actions or reactions were based on something that he knew.

The problem of intuition is related to a general question which may be stated thus:

From what data do human beings form their judgments of reality?

(By *judgment* is meant an image of reality which affects behavior and feelings toward reality. An *image* is formed by integrating sensory and other impressions with each other and with inner tensions based on present needs and past experiences. By *reality* is meant the potentialities for interaction of all the energy systems in the universe; this implies the past.)

Regarding the special matter of concern here, the "primarily subconscious" material which forms the basis for judgments about external reality, Reik (ibid.) has made

5

some formulations with which the present conclusions, based on clinical experimental material, are in agreement. This is all the more impressive since the latter were arrived at independently after the pertinent observations had been made, during: 1) Attempts to intuit a specific kind of characteristic or attribute in several thousand cases. 2) Attempts to intuit whatever possible in single cases.

Curiously enough, among philosophers, the man whose ideas come closest to these conclusions is one of the most ancient. It was Aristotle who described what has been called "intuitive induction" as being based on the ability of the organism, first to experience sense perceptions; at a higher level of organization, to retain sense perceptions; and at a still higher level, to systematize such memories. "We conclude that these states of knowledge are neither innate in a determinate form, nor developed from other higher states of knowledge, but from sense perception. It is like a rout in battle stopped by first one man making a stand and then another, until the original formation has been restored" (from Cohen and Nagel, 1934). It is also apparent how closely Aristotle's remarks are related to the discussion of the similarities between neurophysiological phenomena and the functioning of calculating machines which is part of the subject of cybernetics according to N. Wiener (1948a).

The clinical material has a special bearing on one aspect of this question: Namely, from what data other than rational conclusions and consciously perceived sense impressions do human beings form judgments about external reality? ("Consciously perceived sense impressions" are those which can be readily verbalized, in contrast to "subconscious perceptions" (Hinsie and Shatzky, 1945) and the "subliminal cues" of modern psychology.)

Clinical Material

These observations were made at an army separation center in the latter part of 1945. One part of the processing consisted of a medical examination carried out in assembly-line fashion. Each soldier went down a line of booths, and in each booth certain organ systems were examined and the results noted in the appropriate places on a printed form. The writer was in a booth at the end of the line. The time available for the "psychiatric examination" varied on different days from 40 to 90 seconds. About 25,000 soldiers came down the line in less than four months. Several studies were made during this period, and about 10,000 cases were available for the study of the intuitive process.

The study was not formulated premeditatively. The writer became interested gradually in the nature of the process which with practice enabled him to detect and distinguish accurately some categories of human beings after 10 or 20 seconds of inspection.

The men all wore the same garments, a maroon bathrobe and a pair of cloth slippers. The examiner sat behind a desk, facing the door of the booth. After a soldier was "examined," the appropriate blank was filled in on the form, and the next candidate was summoned by calling "Next!" As one soldier left, the next one shuffled in, and without any instruction, walked toward a chair beside the desk to the right of the examiner and sat down. Some soldiers kept their papers in their hands and some handed them to the examiner. These forms were looked at after the interview was ended. It was not necessary to know the names of the soldiers.

The "examination" consisted of two stock questions which were asked after a few moments of inspection: "Are you nervous?" and "Have you ever been to a psychiatrist?" At first, that was all, unless there were special indications. During this preliminary period, an attempt was made to predict from silent observation of the soldier how each man would answer the two stock questions in that particular situation. It was found that this could be done with surprising accuracy. The question then arose as to how these predictions were made, since this was not immediately apparent. After careful study the question: "How are such intuitive judgments made, and upon what are they based?" was partly answered for the factors concerned.

It seemed evident, however, that the formulation was not completely successful, for the percentage of such correct predictions remained higher when the intuitive process was allowed to function without conscious interference, than when judgments were attempted on the basis of deliberate use of the criteria which had been verbalized. The conclusion drawn was that the criteria used in the intuitive process had not all been formulated. A discussion of the nature of these particular criteria and their psychodynamic and psychiatric implications will not be undertaken here.

When it was thus found almost by accident that the intuitive process could be studied in that particular situation, a more formal experiment was undertaken. An attempt was made to guess by observing the soldier for a few seconds what each man's occupation had been in civilian life, and then to formulate the data upon which the guesses were based. During this experiment, the intuitions regarding the answers to the routine questions about nervousness were forthcoming as well, with practically no additional effort, and continued to be useful in picking out false negative replies. This means that two fields of intuition were active at the same time. Fortunately, then, the experiment did not interfere with the duty of making the best possible psychiatric evaluation of each man in the time available; and, I was informed later, it added interest and spirit to the routinized experience of each man's examination. Since the center was not set up for experimental psychology, no control of the results was possible other than by the individual soldiers who went through the experience, except occasionally during a lax period, when some medical officer from a neighboring booth would drop in.

During the examination, the soldiers were under emotional tension related to a uniform goal; namely, getting out of the army as soon as possible, for they believed that the doctors could frustrate this desire. This tension was particularly high when they entered the psychiatrist's booth, because of the particularly imponderable (in their minds) nature of his function. The interview was an emotionally charged "examination" crisis, and not an artificial laboratory situation. This was emphasized in that environment by the fact that the soldiers were unclothed and were enlisted men, while the examiner was fully clothed and an officer. Upon becoming a participant in this situation, each was met by a neutral but unswerving gaze, and by silence and obvious "observation," in a fashion which only a few, if any of them, could have experienced before. Thus for most of them it was an imponderable, anxiety-laden, and new situation.

Since written protocols were not regularly kept, numerical data are available for only a small sampling of the study. On 17 different days, the guesses or lack of them were recorded for "unselected" segments of the lineup, comprising in all, 391 cases. In 84 of these cases, no attempt was made at guessing the occupation, as no clear impression was obtained by inspection. In the remaining 307 cases, guesses were made and recorded. Of these guesses, 168, or 55 percent, were correct, and 139, or 45 percent, were incorrect. On other days, when intrinsic distractions (as opposed to extraneous stimuli) were operating, as on the day when the separation center was deactivated, only about one-quarter as many correct guesses were made as on the days when intuition was operating, free from relevant emotional interferences: e.g., 14 percent of correct guesses as compared with 55 percent. A similar fall in accuracy usually occurred as fatigue set in, if more than 50 guesses in succession were attempted. It was noted that there was a "learning period" of about two weeks when the study began, during which the reliability of the intuitive process gradually increased, after which no further significant increase was demonstrable.

Records on this subject were spread over a period of 47 days, interspersed with other studies. The following is the first half of a statistically-average record presented verbatim. (The special notes, including those referring to "eye sign," will be discussed later.)

Throughout the study, as exemplified, continual attempts were made to verbalize the grounds for the judgments. Whenever a criterion was satisfactorily verbalized, it was tested on several hundred cases. It was found again, as in the case of diagnosing "neurotic behavior" in the preliminary period, that reliance on such formulated criteria yielded less reliable results than intuition. Each time a new criterion was added to the formulation the percentage of hits went up, but never reached the level attained through the use of intuition during "intuitive periods."

The occupations which were most closely studied were "farmers" and "mechanics." These were the two groups which the examiner became most adept at diagnosing. From the series of 307 guesses which were recorded, 58 out of 79 guesses of "farmer," or 74 percent, were correct, while 14 actual farmers, or 20 percent of their total, were wrongly assigned; and 17 out of 32 guesses of "mechanic," or 53 percent, were correct, with 10 actual mechanics, or 37 percent of their total, wrongly assigned. During the whole run of the experiment, recorded and unrecorded, which included an estimated 2,000 cases, about 50 cases a day for about six weeks, the percentages of correctly recognized farmers and mechanics were high. The study of intuition in connection with these two occupational groups revealed some of the properties of the process. The following formulations gradually emerged, as the basis for each separate judgment was studied.

PROTOCOL NO. 1

7 November 1945

Guess	Inquiry	Notes
1. Truck or factory	Truck or factory	(Short, alert, stocky)
2. Lawyer or small storekeeper	Lawyer	
3. Farmer	Farmer	(Eye sign present)
4. Machinist or truck driver	Truck driver	
5. Farmer	Milkman	(Had suitable complexion but not the eye sign, and I doubted it)
6. No guess made	Ranch and bull stud man	
7. No guess made	Auto body, welding, etc.	
8. Something to do automobiles	Truck driver	

11

Guess	*Inquiry*	*Notes*
9. Truck driver	Truck Driver	(Something about the mouth and the way the hands are held; or wrists?)
10. Farmer	Farmer	(Eye sign)
11. Mechanic	Mechanic and carpenter	(I.e., "uses hands")
12. Sales or office	Farm or factory	(Uncertain soft voice; anxiety state, moderate)
13. Contractor	School teacher	(Handles, i.e., bosses prople)
14. No guess made	Steel mill	
15. Oil fields	Farm	(Retested for eye sign and was positive)
16. Raised on farm, worked in factory later	Raised on farm, worked in factory later	(Eye sign modified)
17. Raised on farm, worked in a big city	Raised on farm, worked in a big city as plumber and mechanic	
18. Truck driver	Truck driver in army, in civilian life was sexton in cemetery	
19. I don't know, probably a mechanic	Logger. Truck driver in army	
20. No guess	Truck driver	
21. Farmer	Truck driver, small town	(Eye sign too fast for farmer)

1. Certain men, when they met the examiner's neutral gaze, shifted their eyes to the left and stared out of the window. The examiner came to call this in his mind the "farmer's eye sign." It was felt, however, that this was not the whole story and that something was being missed; that the intuitive results were based on something more which was being observed and which was not included in this verbalization.

2. This uneasy feeling was confirmed by the fact that when intuition was suspended and this "eye sign" criterion was consciously applied, there were many more errors in determination. A study of these errors led to a refinement and reformulation of the criterion. The true "farmer's eye sign," which was, with few exceptions, peculiar to farmers in the given situation, was found: 1) to occur only in individuals whose faces froze after a few seconds into a stolid expression; and 2) to consist of a special type of gaze-shift to the left, namely, a slow and expressionless one. A rapid shift or an alert expression during the shift was not often seen in members of this occupational group.

This is noted in Case 21, where the erroneous guess of "farmer" was made. The man said that his regular occupation was truck driver, and then it was noted: "Eye sign too fast for farmer." In Case 15, "oil fields" was the guess, but the man said he was a farmer. He was then retested for the farmer's eye sign and it was found to be positive. In the next case, No. 16, the guess was "raised on farm, worked in factory later"; and it was noted that the farmer's eye sign was present in a modified form. The nature of this frequently occurring type of modification was not successfully verbalized.

3. Since the refinement in active observation of the farmer's eye sign still resulted in a lower level of correct hits than did the use of "intuition," other objectively

definable factors were sought. The examiner began to take conscious note of the complexion, which had not been done before. This proved unreliable by itself, but if thoughtfully correlated with the eye sign, it helped in a good many cases, and decreased the negative errors (i.e., guessing something else for a farmer); but it did not decrease the positive errors (i.e., guessing "farmer" in the case of other occupations, as in Case 5). (This result has implications which are not sufficiently important or well-founded with the evidence at hand to warrant discussion.) Since the examiner did not consciously direct his attention to the hands unless he was otherwise baffled, as in Case 9, the extent of their diagnostic influence in this situation is unknown. (Cf. F. Ronchese, 1945.)

In the case of mechanics, the verbalization which gradually took form was as follows:

Certain men, when they met the examiner's gaze, looked straight into his eyes with an expression of lively curiosity, but without challenge. (Because of "challenge," guessing by eye sign was unsuccessful with officers, and the sign was found to be applicable only to enlisted men in this particular situation.*) This group generally proved to be mechanics. Where a positive "mechanic's eye sign" was present but the man said he was not a mechanic, he belonged in many cases to an allied trade, such as radio technician. This observation has its own significance, which can be discussed later.

Men of other occupational groups manifested a variety of eye movements which did not seem to be specifically correlated with their occupations.

The diagnosis of "truck driver" was correct in 22 out of

---

*It was a long time after the event before it occurred to me that "challenge" itself constituted an "officer's eye sign" in the given situation.

36 recorded cases, or 61 percent. It was overlooked 11 times in the 307 recorded cases. Attempts to verbalize in connection with this occupation were made (as in Case 9), but they were not successful. The same applies to construction workers, who were frequently picked out successfully. It was noted that these were often of mesomorphic, or combined athletic-pyknic, physique, but no further clues could be verbalized.

Some of the individual guesses were interesting, in that in a few cases, factors other than occupation were intuited. A passive attitude of mind was maintained, oriented toward "occupation," but it happened occasionally that a man gave such a strong impression concerning some other factor, that "occupation" was heavily overshadowed. This frequently happened in the case of New Yorkers, who, silent in their bathrobes, sometimes gave such a strong impression of being, above all, New Yorkers, that other intuitions seemed to be put in umbrage. There was one professional gambler among the 25,000 men, and he was picked out successfully. Salesmen were picked out with considerable regularity, but only after they had talked, and the notes in such cases are revealing; for example: "Deep voice, good animation—a talker." "Good talker—also they say more than the others, instead of just 'yes' or 'no.'" The verbalized criterion in the case of salesmen was: "If he appears to 'love' his voice, he is most likely a salesman. His voice is important to him as an instrument for dealing with reality." This verbalization has interesting psychodynamic implications.

This observation in the case of salesmen, and further consideration of the occurrence of "eye signs" in farmers and mechanics, gradually led to a new and even startling line of thought which was helpful in the attempt to understand the intuitive process. It was found eventually that in effect it was not occupations at all which were being judged, but attitudes toward reality problems. It appeared that the positive farmer's eye sign did not mean "farmer," so much as "one who waits stolidly in the face of an imponderable situation"; while the positive mechanic's eye sign signified not "mechanic," but "one who is curious to know what will happen next and how things will work out." This accounted for the nature of some of the errors, as in guessing "mechanic" in the case of a radio technician. The question of what heritage, which experiences, and what instinctual constellations conditioned these eye signs, is beyond the present scope.

One may now turn from intuitions based on the manner in which the individual met a novel and anxiety-laden present reality situation to those which had another basis and dealt with other aspects of the individual's personality. From a collection of cases, a few may be selected which are particularly pertinent to the present discussion. These reveal to what extent the subject can communicate information concerning elements with which the intuiter has no direct contact.

PROTOCOL NO. 2

During tours of night duty in various army hospitals, the writer adopted the custom of passing time with patients on the wards whenever opportunity offered. One evening, upon entering an unfamiliar ward, I found a patient who was unknown to me sitting in the office. Knowing that he should not have been there, he rose with an apology; but I felt that he was an interesting and intelligent individual and suggested that he remain. After this brief exchange of politenesses and a few moments of contemplation I ventured to guess, correctly, the city of his birth and the age at which he had left home. The conversation then proceeded as follows:

Case 1.

Q. I believe your mother "disappointed" you.

A. Oh, no, Sir, I love my mother very much.

Q. Where is she now?

A. She's at home. She's not well.

Q. How long has she been ill?

A. Most of her life. I've been taking care of her since I was a young fellow.

Q. What's her trouble?

A. She's always been nervous. A semi-invalid.

Q. Then in that sense, she "disappointed" you, don't you think? She had to take emotional support from you rather than give it to you, from your earliest years.

A. Yes, Sir, that's correct, all right.

At this point another man who was a stranger to me entered the office, and was invited to sit down. He sat on the floor with his back against the wall and said nothing, but listened with great interest.

Q. (To the first man.) You give me the impression that your father was ineffective from the time you were about nine.

A. He was a drunkard. I believe about the time I was nine or 10 he began to drink more heavily.

Case 2.

After listening to a few more such exchanges, the second man requested to be told something about himself.

Q. Well, I think your father was very strict with you. You had to help him on the farm. You never went fishing or hunting with him. You had to go on your own, with a bunch of rather tough fellows.

A. That's right.

Q. He began to scare you badly when you were about seven years old.

A. Well, my mother died when I was six, if that had anything to do with it.

Q. Were you pretty close to her?

A. I was.

Q. So her death left you more or less at the mercy of your father?

A. I guess it did.

Q. You make your wife angry.

A. I guess I did. We're divorced.

This took me by surprise. After a moment we proceeded:

Q. She was about sixteen and a half when you married her.

A. That's right.

Q. And you were about nineteen and a half when you married her?

A. That's right.

Q. Is it right within six months?

A. (Pause.) They're both right within two months.

Q. Well, fellows, that's as far as I can go.

A. Will you try to guess my age?

Q. I don't think I'm in the groove for guessing ages tonight. I think I'm through.

A. Well, try, Sir.

Q. I don't think I'll get this, but I'll try. You were 24 in September.

A. I was 30 in October.

Q. Well, there you are.

About a week later, these men, with their consent, appeared in a clinic designed to demonstrate how the early emotional adventures of the individual leave their marks not only on his later personality, but also on his muscular set, particularly about the face. On that occasion I had an opportunity to learn their names and read their case histories. Some time later one of the men was encountered in civilian life, at which meeting some of the intuitive deductions were reconfirmed. Away from the artificial situations of army life, we are still good friends.

PROTOCOL NO. 3

Case 1.

At the request of two psychiatric colleagues in the army, I interviewed in their presence a new arrival on their ward to ascertain whether the delicate intuitive process could function under conditions of controlled observation. I found that after asking the subject a few "irrelevant" questions in order to get an impression of the dynamics of his voice and facial muscles, it was possible to make some conjectures about his early relationships with his parents, his work history, the destiny of his later relationships, and other factors. It was correctly surmised, for example, that he changed jobs frequently because of misunderstandings with his employers, but that he had finally settled down to a job where he had no one supervising him and had managed to hold this job much longer than any of the others. The important point, however, is not that some of the guesses were correct, but that none of them was incorrect. This incident gave a distinct impression that intuition is sometimes able to function when "put on the spot."

Case 2.

All three of us were interested in pursuing the matter further, and an opportunity presented itself with the arrival of a new patient from another service for psychiatric consultation. The senior psychiatrist made some of the usual anamnestic inquiries of the 27-year-old bachelor, and then asked for my comments. I ventured to say that in my opinion an important precipitating factor in the case was some shock which the man had received at the age of 18. (His adolescence had not been investigated during the previous questioning.) The man stated that nothing serious had happened to him during that period of his life. In spite of his statement, I intimated that the strength of my intuition persisted.

After further questioning, the senior psychiatrist asked him why he had not yet married, whereupon the patient burst into tears, and said:

"I was supposed to be married once, we were all set for a big wedding, and everybody was at church waiting and she never did show up. That was when I was 18 years old, as the captain said. I didn't want to tell you about it."

When the intuitive mood is strong, it brings with it a feeling of certainty which is difficult to shake off. Just as the man in Case 1, Protocol No. 2, denied that his mother had "disappointed" him, so this man stated that nothing serious had happened to him at the age of 18; yet further questioning in both cases confirmed the intuitive impression.

PROTOCOL NO. 4

Many years ago, after some "irrelevant" conversation with a young woman whose existence I had no reason previously to suspect, I made the following observation.

Q. I have the feeling that you are either the fourth or the seventh of 11 children.

A. I am the fourth of 11 children and I have seven brothers.

This confirmation was apparently more incredible to me than my observation was to the individual in question. Other sources later corroborated her statement. My remark was preceded by a feeling which might be roughly translated as follows: "If I watch this person closely for a few moments something might occur to me."

PROTOCOL NO. 5

During the war, while talking to a young woman who was previously unknown to me, I advanced the hypothesis that she had 28 teeth. This hypothesis was based on a sudden "inspiration" which came to me at that moment without any premeditation. She had not shown her teeth, and my observation, including the number 28, was irrelevant to anything we had discussed, except possibly her sadistic tendencies; nor am I in the habit of enumerating people's teeth. She herself did not think that my comment was accurate, but we reviewed the situation and found that it was.

One is sometimes astonished at the accuracy of intuition as exemplified in the last two protocols and others like them. One would expect, if one guessed "number" in a large series of cases, to be right in a certain proportion; it is quite another thing to be right almost all the time when in a certain frame of mind. I have observed that when the intuition seems strong enough to risk a guess of "number," the guess is nearly always accurate. When the "intuitive mood" is not present, or when intuition is "put on the spot," guesses of numbers are more likely to be erroneous, as in Case 2, Protocol No. 2. In this case, while intuition was functioning spontaneously it was possible to guess correctly the age of a man's unseen wife when he married her; when the mood left, and in the face of a challenge, there was a gross error in guessing the age of the man who stood there in person.

It is true that unless one actively cultivates intuition at times, such incidents occur only a few times a year. One must control one's attitude toward such matters. Intuition might be used in practice to make an estimate of a patient's personality, an estimate which would become clouded as it was overlaid with clinical material; usually one would find in the end, however, when this "clouded" period had been worked through, that the first intuition was reliable. It is probably detrimental, however, either to record one's intuitions in ordinary practice or to communicate them to the patient. Such an externalization tends to limit the fluidity of images which is desirable for the best therapeutic results. If one makes a restricted and carefully thought-out communication in this regard to two or three patients for experimental purposes, one easily becomes convinced that such comments are not taken lightly and may have a far-reaching effect on the therapeutic situation. On the other hand, with strangers it is necessary first to establish the proper rapport if one wishes to exercise such privileges; otherwise difficulties may no doubt arise.

Qualities of the Intuitive Function

A certain attitude of mind, the "intuitive mood," is most favorable to the intuitive function. Little was learned by the writer about the "psychic environment" which was most conducive to such a mood. Extraneous stimuli need not necessarily be excluded. The soldiers at the separation center were examined in a chilly open booth in a noisy atmosphere of hurry and excitement, and the examiner was able to engage in conversation with colleagues between the short periods of concentration which lasted a few seconds each. Such notes on the protocols as: "Room very chilly today," were not followed by any diminution in accuracy. Neither were such notes as: "Up a good part of the night last night," so that the relevance of known (extraneous) internal stimuli is a question which needs further study. On the other hand, the note: "Separation center deactivated today," was followed by a serious loss of intuitive efficiency.

Knowledge of the conditions required to induce the intuitive mood at will would be of great value, but unfortunately no one has yet been able to verbalize these conditions. Such a mood does not resemble the state of withdrawal from reality which advanced students of Yoga, and others, are able to attain, since it is possible during intuitive periods to maintain normal relationships with psychiatrists and other individuals. Perhaps a narrowed and concentrated contact with external reality is necessary. The chief requisite seems to be a state of alertness and receptiveness, requiring, however, more intense concentration and more outwardly directed attention than the passively alert state which is familiar to psychotherapists.

Directed participation of the perceptive ego interfered with intuition. When previously verbalized sensory clues were deliberately sought, the intuitive process was impaired, although it could be immediately resuscitated. This may have some psychodynamic connection with my experience that clinical intuition works poorly with acquaintances of the "intuiter" and functions best with complete strangers. Deutsch (1944, p. 136) remarks that intuition "will naturally depend on one's sympathy and love for and spiritual affinity with the other person," but I have found that in general a previous acquaintance with the subject is an obstacle to be overcome and not an asset. In special cases, however, where the "clouded period" referred to in the foregoing has been successfully worked through in either a professional or a personal relationship, her statement takes on its true connotations. The problem of resistance is still to be clarified in this connection.* (Cf. Pederson-Krag, 1947.) Similar factors probably tend to hamper intuition when the intuiter is "put on the spot." He needs a mechanism for dealing with any anxiety aroused by such a situation, or his intuition is likely to fail, even if the subject himself is a stranger.

With practice, the intuitive mood can be attained more easily. Unless one is in good form, it is difficult to become intuitive at will. Many psychiatrists and psychoanalysts successfully use intuition day after day when they are in active practice, but sometimes after a vacation period find their intuition "rusty." Specialists in other professions who work partly by intuition often find after a holiday that while they may return with fresh mind and viewpoint, their intuition is not so effective as before until they are

---

*It was resistance and countertransference which blinded me at first to the fact that "challenge" was a diagnostic sign for officers in the given situation, and made me feel instead that it was an obstacle. Detailed analysis of this interesting insight is beyond the present scope.

back in the swing of their usual practice again. A similar example is the regular daily working of intuition at the separation center, and the sporadic occurrence of the intuitive mood when it was not in daily use.

The intuitive function is fatigable; e.g., after about 50 successive guesses at the separation center, the percentage of correct guesses fell off markedly. And despite the subjectively observed inactivity of some of the ego functions, intuition is fatiguing. The type of fatigue may be compared to that felt after any difficult mental strain, such as a hard game of chess.

There was considerable evidence that the accuracy of the impressions improved with accumulated experience in each field, but the possibility of a plateau effect once it reached a certain level could not be eliminated. The case of the woman with 28 teeth, as well as other cases, raises the question of whether extensive previous experience in a given field is always a prerequisite for intuitive accuracy. It was interesting to note that accuracy was not diminished when judgments were sought in two different fields at the same time (e.g., "degree of neuroticism" and "occupational group"), so that intuitions do not seem to interfere with each other.

Some of these conditions are reminiscent of those mentioned by Rhine for what he calls the "extrasensory perception" function. The conditions outlined here may be summarized as follows:

The intuitive mood is enhanced by an attitude of alertness and receptiveness without actively directed participation of the perceptive ego. It is attained more easily with practice; it is fatigable, and fatiguing. Intuitions in different fields do not seem to interfere with each other. Intuitions are not all dependent upon extensive past experience in the given field. Extraneous physical stimuli, both exter-

nal and internal, appear to be irrelevant. *

Some self-observation during the intuitive process yielded a kind of introspective formula which can be stated as follows:

Things are being "automatically" arranged just below the level of consciousness; "subconsciously perceived" factors are being sorted out, fall "automatically" into place, and are integrated into the final impression, which is at length verbalized with some uncertainty. *

Again one is reminded of the recent cybernetic formulations.

The more prolonged the gaze, the greater the amount of the material which seemed to go through the process, and the greater the number of the impressions which could be verbalized. When the perceptive ego was not directed, the activity of some other function could be "felt," and the fatigue of this latter function could be sensed if an attempt was made to continue too long.

What Is Intuited?

We have evidence that an intuition consists of two processes: a "subconscious perception," and a conscious verbalization. At the separation center, the conscious verbalizations were at first naively accepted as formulations of the actual intuitions. It was thought that the intuitive function was actually perceiving "occupational group." Later it became apparent that what the intuitive function really perceived was "attitude toward an imponderable reality situation." The intuiter's ego then translated these perceptions into a judgment concerning occupational group.

With the men on the ward (Protocol No. 2) a similar

---

*Italics by the editor of this reprinting.

process took place. For example, one verbalization consisted of: "She was about sixteen and a half when you married her," and it was thought that this was what was intuited. Actually, in retrospect, the preconscious material was felt to have run about as follows: "This is a man who lacked feminine influence in later childhood and wanted to get away from his father. Such a man as I see before me married young and impulsively, choosing a wife on the basis of certain needs and anxieties of the moment. In this type of case she would be a few years younger than himself and as 'lost' as himself. (Ergo, he married a girl who was ready to get married at the age of sixteen and a half.)"

Later, the corollary to this was formulated on the basis of the intuition, "The situation came to a head in late adolescence," and was verbalized as follows: "He married when he was nineteen and a half years old." (In this case the actual ages have been changed slightly for reasons of discretion.)

We are led to believe that there are at least two types of factors which may be intuited: attitudes toward reality, and instinctual vicissitudes; or more succinctly, ego attitudes and id attitudes. These may be verbalized into guesses, for example, of occupational group and object choice, respectively.

There seemed to be specific clues related to each of these factors. The subject's attitude toward an imponderable reality situation was usually gauged primarily from clues supplied by the eyes and the periocular muscles. I believe that impressions concerning the instincts and their vicissitudes were largely based on "subconscious observation" of the muscles of the lower face, especially of those about the mouth. Head posture, and mannerisms based on tonus of the neck muscles can also be indicators in this respect. One might say that in these situations the eyes were principally instruments of the ego, while the mouth and neck were more expressive of the functions of the id.

Discussion

The material presented here has offered an opportunity to discuss, supported by a number of clinical examples, ideas which have been the subject of speculation for many centuries. In attempting to place these findings in a broader frame of reference one arrives at viewpoints similar to those of Bergson (ibid.) and Reik (ibid.): Standing on the small island of the intellect, many are trying to understand the sea of life; at most we can understand only the flotsam and jetsam, the flora and fauna which are cast upon the shores. Taking a verbal or mechanical microscope to what we find will help but little to know what lies beyond the horizon or in the depths. For this we must swim or dive, even if the prospect dismays us at first.

To understand intuition, it seems necessary to avoid the belief that in order to know something the individual must be able to put into words what he knows and how he knows it. This belief, still common since Freud, is the result of what appears to be an overdevelopment of reality testing, which tempts some who are interested in psychology to think too far away from nature and the world of natural happenings. Dogs know things, and so do bees (von Frisch, Lubbock), and even *stentor* (Jennings). True knowledge is to know how to act rather than to know words. If a certain man looks out of the window in a certain way, we may know how to behave toward that man and what to expect from him. If another man looks at us with lively curiosity, we may know how to behave toward and what to expect from him. To put what we know about these men into words is quite another matter. The relationship of such matters to intragroup reactions (i.e., through what mediums other than words do people provoke and communicate with each other) and to the "undirected function" of the central nervous system (Federn, 1938) remains to be clarified.

In attempting to "isolate" operations, particularly operations of the human mind, one is reminded that the concept, "isolation of an operation," is itself a creation of the human mind. Since the mind is in such cases attempting to think about itself with itself as an instrument, a difficulty arises allied to the kind of difficulty which in logic is typified by Epimenides (cf. B. Russell's discussions of "paradoxes"). Just as some statements about propositions must be analyzed differently from other classes of propositions, so mentation about mental phenomena may be considered differently from mentation about other natural phenomena. The future of psychology may lie in the paradoxes rather than in the body of logic. (Cf. the modern methodological approaches of Einstein, H. Weyl, Korzybski, N. Wiener, et al.)

In a previous publication (1947, pp. 279-286), in which some of the material studied in this paper is mentioned briefly, I summarized the problem along the following lines: In subduing the forces of the id, man often imprisons much that could be useful and beneficial to the individual. Many people could cultivate intuitive faculties without endangering the rest of their personalities and their necessary testing of reality.*

---

*On the contrary, my initial failure to recognize "challenge" as a diagnostic sign for officers was evidence of involvement with my own questionable anxieties of the moment; the subsequent recognition of the intuitive value of this phenomenon represented freedom and insight and improved reality testing.

Freud felt confident enough to imply that there is no need to be alarmed by proposals of this nature (1933, p. 80). One might even go so far as to agree that in everyday life we learn more, and more truly, through intuition than we do through verbalized observations and logic. We are tempted to be proud of verbalizations, but it is possible that in many of our most important judgments the small and fragile voice of intuition is a more reliable guide.

Wittels has outlined the weakness of intuition (1945): "1) one has to be endowed with it, 2) it may lead us astray, 3) soon a definite limit is reached beyond which there is no further progress without scientific method. I have never met a man who could equal Freud in intuition, i.e., of inexplicable immediate psychological insight. But he also had scientific self-control which—with a few exceptions—did not trust his unproved visions." To which an optimistic man might reply: 1) that he believes everyone is endowed with intuition and needs only to get at it; 2) that it will not lead us astray if we can free it from destructive involvement with neurotic constellations and anxieties; and 3) (Poincaré, ibid.) that there is a time for scientific method and a time for intuition—the one brings with it more certainty, the other offers more possibilities; the two together are the only basis for creative thinking.

Conclusions

1. An intuitive function exists in the human mind.

2. Under proper conditions, this function can be studied empirically.

3. The intuitive function is part of a series of perceptive processes which work above and below the level of consciousness in an apparently integrated fashion, with shifting emphasis according to special conditions.

4. The clinical intuitions studied were found in most cases to be based at least partly on preconscious, sensory observations of the subject.

5. What is intuited is different from what the "intuiter" verbalizes as his intuition.

6. The dynamics of the eyes and the periocular muscles express reality attitudes. The dynamics of the lower facial and neck muscles are more indicative of instinctual vicissitudes.

7. Intuitive faculties may be more important than is often admitted in influencing judgments about reality in everyday life.

8. The intuitive function is useful and worth cultivating.

2 Concerning the Nature of Diagnosis

Diagnosis by Inspection

EVERY HUMAN BEING is to some extent capable of establishing a diagnosis by inspection. Even mentally dull individuals can distinguish between a 10-year-old child and a 20-year-old man. Most adults can work with a smaller difference threshold, such as distinguishing between a 30-year-old and a 40-year-old in the majority of trials. A clinician likes to think he can do better than that. Some physicians become very skillful in this respect, and can usually guess the age of a patient under 40 accurately to within two years. The writer has seen talented experts repeatedly conjecture adults' ages correctly to within three months. Age-guessers at carnivals are willing to bet on their accuracy, and come out very well in large series of cases.

There are several aspects to such diagnostic processes which are worth discussing, particularly the preverbal functions involved. Perhaps the simplest example is that of a dull individual who reveals by his behavior that he distinguishes between a 10-year-old and a 20-year-old. In such a case there are several possibilities.

1. The individual may not be aware that he is judging the subjects' ages and guiding his behavior accordingly. If

he is asked, he may even reply in the negative. That is, he is not even aware that he knows something.

2. If he becomes aware that he is behaving differently towards the two subjects, he may not know why. That is, he becomes aware that he knows something but does not know what it is that he knows.

3. If he realizes that he is treating the two subjects differently because of the difference in their ages, then he knows that he knows something about them, and knows what it is that he knows, but he may still be unable to say *how* he knows it.

4. If he tries to explain *how* he knows it, his explanation is likely to be unsatisfactory both to him and to the listener.

In this case, the individual behaves as though he had made a diagnosis, but he may be quite unaware that he has made it. If he is aware, he may be unaware of what it is that he has diagnosed; if he is aware of that, he may be unable to justify his diagnosis, and if he attempts to do so, his justification may not be convincing.

A more subtle example in some ways is that of the clinician who decides before asking that a certain patient is 36 years old. This clinician knows that he knows something, he knows what it is that he knows, and he is able to say in a general way how he knows it. He may say that his diagnosis is based on careful inspection of the individual's face; or he may say that it is the fruit of free-floating, undirected attention. If he is asked, however, to formulate his criteria for differentiating a 30-year-old from a 39-year-old, he will usually confess his inability to do so.

A carnival weight-guesser recently tried to formulate his diagnostic criteria (Mygatt, 1947). These criteria may be useful within a 50-pound margin of permissible error, but they give no convincing indication of how he could guess weights accurately to within five pounds, as these people can readily do with a very high percentage of accuracy. His exposition seems to be a rationalization of his diagnoses rather than a basis for them.

It is apparent, therefore, that there are cognitive processes which function below the level of consciousness. In fact, human beings, when they are in full possession of their faculties, behave at all times as though they were continually and quickly making very subtle judgments about their fellowmen without being aware that they are doing so; or if they are aware of what they are doing, without being aware of *how* they do it. If they try to verbalize these processes, their explanations are too crude to account for the refinement of the judgments, even among professionals who are continually trying to formulate diagnostic criteria. Their explanations seem to be rationalizations of their diagnoses, rather than expositions of the real diagnostic process.

Psychiatrists, for example, are continually making accurate diagnoses all over the world, yet it is a noteworthy accomplishment for one of them to formulate in words a useful diagnostic criterion; even then, such a criterion has to be hedged with cautions and exceptions. Although each such formulation may be helpful in a small way, in essence the preliminary diagnosis of an experienced clinician is a product of preverbal processes which are functions of his skill, keenness, and experience, rather than the result of the deliberate application of a collection of formal criteria. It appears that the most important judgments which human beings make concerning each other are the products of preverbal processes—cognition without insight—which function almost automatically below the level of consciousness. In the case of age diagnosis and in many other cases as well, it can be readily shown that the

35

subconscious processes are more accurate, refined, and reliable than conscious diagnostic processes. Nevertheless, a certain restraint deprives many people of the free use of this valuable faculty.

Verbalizing Diagnostic Criteria

During the last war Professor Eugen Kahn, in a private conversation, made a remark to the effect that it is possible for an alert and experienced psychiatrist to pick out men unfit for military service very rapidly in the setting of an induction center, and that detailed study of inductees would add comparatively little to such a psychiatrist's percentage of accuracy.* This statement was given a modest test by the writer at the first opportunity, and it was found that after a preliminary period of practice it was possible to make certain judgments in a minimum period of time with considerable accuracy.

A preliminary study was made at an induction center where the clerical staff administered the Cornell Selectee Index. It was found possible to estimate closely in a large number of cases the score of each candidate by looking at him for a few seconds before turning over the sheet to see what his score was. It was found that the estimates were correct to within three points in a large percentage of cases, even including those whose scores lay between 15 and 25. This was taken to mean that the inductee revealed by a few seconds of spontaneous behavior in the specific situation characteristics which were correlated with his score on the questionnaire.

After this . . . [the previously described] attempt was

---

*Quoted by permission.

made to predict, after a few moments of looking in each case, the responses of [the] several thousand soldiers to the . . . two questions:

1. Are you nervous?
2. Have you ever been to a psychiatrist?

. . . In a rough way this was a guess as to "how neurotic" the individual was. It was found after a few weeks when a plateau of accuracy had been attained that the guesses were uniformly correct, with only a few exceptions: that is, in a few cases where the guess was "yes," the answer was "no"; and in a few cases where the guess was "no," the answer was "yes." (When a similar and more carefully controlled [written] series was discussed with the late Dr. Paul Federn, he made the surprising remark that the percentages of error in both directions seemed high to him.) Since the records were incomplete, no figures are offered, nor are they essential to the spirit of this study.

An attempt was made to formulate the criteria upon which the predictions were based. It seemed evident that the formulation was not completely successful, for the percentage of such correct predictions remained higher when the "intuitive" process was allowed to function without conscious interference than when judgments were attempted on the basis of deliberate use of the criteria which had been verbalized. The conclusion was drawn that the criteria used in the "intuitive" process had not all been formulated. Those which were formulated, however, could be applied deliberately with much success. The attempt to formulate the nature of the intuitive process itself has [already] been described. . . .

The verbalized diagnostic criteria formed the basis for dividing the soldiers into three groups.

1. One group of soldiers would meet the

psychiatrist's eye squarely and answer the ensuing questions in a clear, firm voice. Many of them would smile at him before the questions were asked and a good many of them after answering, in an engaging and friendly fashion, which provoked the designation of "a well-integrated reaction." The psychiatrist, having just spent a long tour of duty dealing with hospitalized neurotics, had the subjective impression: "These men have nothing to hide," which was in contrast to his impression of the neurotics, who retrospectively began to seem "as though they had something to hide." During the few seconds of silent observation, the men in this group sat in a fairly relaxed fashion without making purposeless movements. They nearly all answered the two questions negatively, and the examiner began to consider that men who behaved in this way were "normal." Since they had all been through one to five years of military service and stated that they did not feel "nervous" at the end and had not consulted or been sent to a psychiatrist during this period, they were loosely considered—at face value—to have demonstrated adequate personality integration in the military situation.

2. A second category of men, when they sat down and were greeted with silence, would make "purposeless" movements, usually of a rhythmic nature, such as swinging their crossed legs; or their gaze would wander to and from the examiner and finally become fixed on some nearby object or some part of their own bodies; or they would finally meet the examiner's eyes in an uncertain fashion. This type of reaction nearly always involved movements of decreasing amplitude, slowly coming to rest, so that they gave the impres-

sion of being "pendular" in quality.

Men in this category also usually gave negative replies to the two stock questions. It was noted after some study that positive replies came from this group nearly always when "the pendulum took longer than usual to come to rest," so that this type of reaction had to be considered in four dimensions rather than in three.

Other positive replies came when the movements were observed to be of unusual amplitude.

3. A third group of men reacted to the situation by making "purposeless," apparently largely "unconscious," movements, which differed from those observed in the previous group in lacking the "pendular" quality. Some of them tried to meet the psychiatrist's gaze, lowered their eyes, and began to tap with their fingers on their thighs or on the desk, or to twist their hands and fingers. Some of them looked around the room and never attempted to meet the psychiatrist's eye. Some of them would start to smile in an uncertain fashion, change their minds, lower their gaze, and begin to fidget or squirm. Most of them did not even attempt to smile; those who did faltered. In other cases, tremors would begin or become worse if present initially. They usually did not answer questions in a clear, firm voice but in a restrained, weak, timid tone.

Members of this group usually answered either one or both of the stock questions in the affirmative, and there appeared to be a correlation between the amount of energy expended "purposely" and the number of questions answered in the affirmative. The more energy they expended in this way, the more likely they were to say that they had been to a psychiatrist, even when they said that they were not "nervous" at the moment.

In some cases where no such "purposeless" expenditures of energy were obvious, the psychiatrist mentally placed the men in the first category and found that he had made an error; i.e., some men who did not appear to make "purposeless" expenditures of energy did say that they were nervous or had been to a psychiatrist. Many of these said they had consulted the psychiatrist for "stomach trouble." Closer observation revealed that these men were expending energy "purposelessly," not by overt movements but through an abnormal increase in muscular tonus; i.e., they were sitting still but they were very tense.

The utilization of energy by these men, especially those in the first and third groups, who under the clinical circumstances constituted the "normal" and the "neurotic" groups respectively, is worth considering briefly.

In the "normal" group the energy activated by the stimulus of the interview was all or nearly all channelized into useful and well-integrated activity, giving force and firmness to the voice. Part of it in many cases found expression in a friendly smile. Little or none of it was manifested in "purposeless" activity. These men were able to communicate directly with the examiner.

In the "neurotic" group, a large part of the activated energy was "misdirected" during the preliminary period of sitting. This "neurotic" activity appeared to be purposeless and autistic, neither friendly nor hostile. But to a professional observer it inadvertently communicated anxiety or hostility. Psychologically, the "purposeless" movements seemed to be distorted kicks, blows, and hostile oral grimaces.

It is noteworthy that in both groups the facial muscles might come into play. Among the "normals," the facial muscles were used as overt instruments of a frank "object relationship," that is, to communicate a friendly feeling to a new human being by smiling. Among the "neurotics," these muscles were used in an autistic way; e.g., for mouth twitchings, which did not directly communicate anything to the other person concerned, except insofar as he was a professional observer.

On another plane of verbalization, the "normals" gave the impression of being happy and of having nothing to hide, while the "neurotics" gave the impression of being unhappy and of having something to hide.

Quantitatively speaking, the psychiatrist would say that the meeting with him was related to a certain expenditure of energy. In "normal" individuals, this found free and more or less full expression in organized, efficient, and tension-relieving activity. In "neurotic" individuals, for reasons which were specific to each individual, it did not, and instead manifested itself in disorganized, inefficient, and unsatisfying activity. In the intermediate group, anxiety also took precedence, and among the more neurotic members of this group it presented a problem which could not be solved in the allotted time.

Further discussion along these lines would go beyond the present scope. It must be emphasized that these soldiers were reacting to a certain individual who greeted them in a certain way. Another individual who greeted them in another way would certainly obtain a different series of responses, as would the same individual who greeted them in another way. In the opinion of the writer the essence of the situation was the neutral, unswerving gaze which left the soldier for the first few seconds without any indication of what he was *supposed* to do.

Diagnosis as a Configurational Process

This experience in the rapid "diagnosis" of large numbers of individuals demonstrated that the intuitive processes which function below the level of consciousness are susceptible of study under certain conditions. Such subconscious processes of cognition are continually at work in human beings and are of importance in everyday living and of theoretical interest in professional work. Biologically, intuition may be related to primitive cognitive processes in lower animals (Darwin, 1886; Krogh, 1948; Wiener, 1948b). Phylogenetically, it preceded verbal knowledge and communication (Sturtevant, 1947, p. 48), and ontogenetically as well (Deutsch, 1944; Schilder, 1942, p. 247). Psychologically, it is important because it is related to problems of group behavior and their limiting case, "what happens between two people," which is the nuclear problem of everyday living and of psychotherapeutic technique. It must be taken into account in formulating the psychological aspects of communication theory, which are becoming ever more important as mathematicians and engineers need assistance from psychology in elaborating their theories of communication (Brillouin, 1950).

Of the many ramifications of this subject, only three will be considered here. First, why is it that such important cognitive processes have been so little studied? The modern literature is limited, consisting mainly of the work of H. Bergson (1944), C. G. Jung (1946), T. Reik (1948), and K. W. Wild (1938). It is noticeable that many people find intuition a disagreeable topic to discuss, and their attitudes may have some of the qualities of a dynamic resistance. Bergson has discussed such attitudes from the philosophical point of view, while W. Kohler (1929) has discussed in another connection similar attitudes rationalized on methodological grounds. People often act as though they are afraid to admit that they know something when they cannot explain to themselves exactly how they know it. We humans sometimes feel more secure if we deny the existence of certain cognitive processes, when we cannot convince ourselves that we have complete insight into them.

Secondly, it is possible to study the development of intuitive processes in a particular field, and a systematic research into this aspect of the matter might be undertaken. In the case of psychiatric diagnosis, certain statements can be made. There are three phases in the development of this skill. With beginners, it is an additive process based on didactic criteria: a series of consciously directed observations is consciously sorted in accordance with formal notions, in an attempt to find a close match among preconceived schemes, in such a way that the whole process can be verbalized for the benefit of the teacher. With experienced clinicians, both the process of observing and the process of sorting and matching are more plastic and complex, and take place partly below the threshold of consciousness. This is the psychologic difference between an amateur and a professional. In the third phase, which verifies and controls the others, the diagnosis is first made plastically below the level of consciousness, and later a secondary process of verbalization and rationalization takes place.

Thirdly, verbal processes are additive, while intuitive processes are integrative. The student in a new field knows no more and no less about that field than he is able to verbalize in the first place. He states his observations and synthesizes them into a diagnosis. The experienced clinician, on the other hand, verbalizes certain aspects which he analytically dissects out of his initial intuitive picture of the patient, which is largely a function of his past experience in the field. In psychologic terms, the student builds up a mosaic, while the experienced clinician tears down a configuration.

The configurational quality of the preliminary intuitive diagnosis can be demonstrated in various ways. In whatever manner the diagnostic processes are categorized, one factor remains constant: these processes are based on observation of the patient or, more precisely, on the understanding of his communications. Many clinicians will agree that the more direct the communications, the more accurate the preliminary diagnosis will be. Most clinicians feel more confident after seeing a new patient in the office than after talking to him "indirectly" over the telephone. Similarly, they prefer to make a diagnosis by interview rather than by mail, even in the case of psychotics. Evidently something happens during various processes of filtration which make many clinicians feel more or less insecure even with a considerable amount of such indirect communication at their disposal. In effect, the clinician tends to feel most secure in his diagnosis when he can observe the total configuration of the patient's personality without the intervention of filters.

In such examples, the filtration processes are obvious to those concerned. The clinician is fully aware that something has been subtracted from the total configuration of the patient's behavior by the communication through an extraneous medium. Not all clinicians, however, are fully aware of the internal systems which may filter their observations and subtract from the material available for the diagnostic processes. The student, for example, may not be actively aware how much his observations are being filtered through the schemata he has learned from teachers and books. Many more experienced clinicians may not be fully cognizant of every aspect of the scheme of countertransference, anxiety, and self-mistrust which nature places between us and our patients. Under such conditions, the diagnostic processes have to work partly with indirect communications strictly speaking. This may account for some of the consistent trends among the participants in psychiatric staff conferences, where one individual may habitually lean toward the diagnosis of depression, another may favor the diagnosis of schizophrenia, while a third may emphasize "psychopathy." Each experienced participant is usually right somehow or other, and obviously each filters differently what he observes. The point here is that he also filters what he is trying to tell himself; that is, intuition has to filter through an arranging ego.

A more specific example of the configurational nature of the intuitive diagnostic process is contained in the following observation. The writer has observed that, when he works in a new office, he is not so sure of himself in the preliminary diagnostic phase as he is in his old office.* It is as though he had to see the patient against a background which had become standardized in his mind before he felt confident that he understood the case. Thus the patient is not the whole configuration concerned in the diagnostic process but is part of a configuration, and it is easier to understand him when he is seen against a well-known background and makes his communications from this background. It appears that this background is an important factor in the more subtle aspects of diagnosis. Yet in defending the diagnosis verbally, the role of the background can only incidentally be formulated. It may be mentioned how the patient used the background, what remarks he made about it, and so forth, but actually the significant diagnostic factor is not the formulation of how

---

*The writer has also observed that there are three major phases in changing the ego boundaries to include a new environment, and that these phases develop after 5 or 6 days, 39 to 45 days, and about 180 days, respectively, in his own case and in many other cases which he has studied in this regard. But this is a different aspect of the problem.

the patient uses the background but the subconscious perception of how he fits into it as part of a configuration. The diagnosis seems to be made "for me" by some cultivated faculty which operates on the whole configuration below the level of consciousness; what is formally called "making the diagnosis," that is, explaining the grounds for it, is only a secondary additive process, justifying what is partly known in some other way, through preconscious and unconscious cognitive process.

Careful consideration reveals another interesting fact. The subconscious process does not really make a diagnosis. It makes a preverbal judgment of the configuration, knowing nothing of diagnostic terminology. What happens is that this judgment is verbalized in diagnostic terminology. For example, [when] the writer . . . tried to guess by inspection the occupations of . . . [the soldiers, he] was quite successful in picking out farmers and mechanics. Careful study revealed, however, that the subconscious process was actually not judging "occupation," but the attitudes of the men toward reality problems, and that assigning them to certain occupational groups was a secondary process based on the intuitive, unverbalized perception of these attitudes; this accounted for some of the apparent errors in verbal judgment.

It appears that verbalizing knowledge is different from knowing about something. Special training in any field is directed toward consciously increased selectivity in scanning configurations, and refinement of verbalization, but these are secondary processes, and the primary perceptive processes take place below the level of consciousness. When the purposeful scanning becomes integrated with the total personality through training and experience, it too takes place below the threshold of consciousness, and this integration leads to greater confidence in stating the results of the scanning. The scanning itself gradually becomes integrative rather than additive. Much of the scanning is conditioned by early experiences, so that different individuals integrate different constellations of qualities and potentialities in observing the people they meet. Later experiences, however, such as professional training, can bring about a similar integrating ability concerned with new constellations.

Psychologically speaking, an amateur in any field becomes a professional when his scanning processes sink below the level of consciousness and function in an integrative rather than an additive fashion. The analogies in the field of motor activity help clarify the point. A beginner dances the rhumba by remembering to put one foot here, then one foot here, and so on, and by this additive process he gets along in an awkward way. After a while he no longer needs to remember, and as a result he dances a smooth, well-integrated rhumba without thinking about it. If he is called upon to explain how he does it, however, he reverts to his former system temporarily.

Comment

The reaction to this presentation usually follows certain lines to which the ensuing comments are relevant.

Since complete records were not kept at the separation center, the number-minded are invited to consider the ideas offered in this report independently of the experience with soldiers. The personality-minded, who might ask what kind of an individual would be interested in such problems, are referred to Sir William Osler, who once made a remark to the effect that a good diagnostician can make a likely preliminary diagnosis by the very way the patient knocks on the door. The idea-minded will be familiar with Bertand Russell's detailed epistemological discussions. Empirically, the fact remains that some individuals, such as professional weight-guessers and experienced clinicians, are better than others at making various kinds of quick judgments about people, depending upon their skill, experience, interest, and receptivity. The writer believes that many people are endowed with much more ability in this regard than they may care to admit. There is no need to bring up questions of "mental telepathy" on the one hand, nor of "summation of subliminal cues" on the other, since the problem can be taken care of in a formal way on the basis of configurational judgments without invoking either extrasensory or additive processes.

Summary

Every normal individual is able to make diagnoses by inspection. Diagnostic processes, such as those concerning age, are preverbal and take place below the level of consciousness. The individual may not be aware that he is diagnosing, or if he is, he may not be aware of how he does it. Attempts to explain diagnostic processes are often only justifications, and only occasionally offer criteria which are useful to other diagnosticians with different personalities, at least in the field of psychology. A series is offered to demonstrate the process of diagnosis by inspection in the psychiatric field, and the diagnostic processes are analyzed as far as they became apparent. The development of diagnostic abilities and a frequently occurring reluctance to trust intuitive knowledge are discussed. Preliminary diagnostic processes in experienced clinicians are based on the analysis of configurations below the level of consciousness, and not, as in beginners, on the conscious synthesis of mosaics of observations.

3 Concerning the Nature of Communication

Cybernetics and Psychiatry

THE PHYSICAL AND ENGINEERING aspects of control devices, calculators, and communication systems (Berkeley, 1949), are now related to a body of precise theory (Shannon & Weaver, 1949). This science, which has been called cybernetics, (Wiener, 1948a) is gradually expanding into territory which is familiar from another point of view to psychologists, psychiatrists, and psychoanalysts. Cybernetics leads from consideration of physical devices like telegraph cables to attempts at precise mathematical analysis of such formulations as, for example, the following: "numerous observations —comparison—thinking—scientific laws—practical application of these laws—new apparatus or machines built" (Brillouin, 1950).

The inspection of such a sequence makes it clear that students of mental science have a pertinent interest in these developments. Communication theory has a great deal to say about the mechanics of certain operations at which living organisms are peculiarly adept, especially in connection with the ability to respond selectively to signals received (Shannon, 1950; Rashevsky, 1938). Cybernetics has hitherto received relatively little attention in the psychiatric literature, although a good deal of discussion by clinicians is mentioned or found in sources not ordinarily consulted by clinicians (Wiener, 1948a, pp. 26 ff.; Symposium, 1948). Some physiologists have actually constructed cybernetic mechanisms as representatives of brain function (Ashby, 1950; Walter, 1950, 1951). Shannon (1950) proposes a chess-playing machine. Meanwhile, the psychological aspects of communication have aroused considerable interest (Bateson & Ruesch, 1951).* But the number of fortunate poeple who have had both intensive training in the theory and practice of communication engineering and extensive experience in dynamic psychotherapy appears to be stringently limited. The specialist in either field hesitates to venture as a layman into the other because of the pitfalls which tempt the uninitiated in such complex matters. Nevertheless it seems worthwhile to run some risks for the sake of scientific empiricism.

Some "cyberneticists" mention or even emphasize the analogies between their machines and the brain, or even the mind: "The realization that the brain and the computing machine have much in common may suggest new and valid approaches to psychopathology, and even to psychiatrics" (Wiener, 1948a, p. 168). Others stress the essential differences: "Active thinking has been done by the designers of the machine and is done by the staff of scientists using the machine. Creative thinking is not to be found in the machinery itself" (Brillouin, 1950).

Cyberneticists, coming in one direction from theoretical physics and practical experience with communication systems and calculating machines, are able to state: "The

---

*Dr. W. R. Ashby of Gloucester, England, conducted the meeting on cybernetics at the International Congress of Psychiatry in Paris in 1950. At this meeting, which was attended by a group with quite heterogeneous viewpoints, little inclination was shown to discuss the subject from the psychological point of view.

information carried by a precise message in the absence of a noise is infinite. In the presence of a noise, however, this amount of information is finite, and it approaches 0 [zero] very rapidly as the noise increases in intensity" (Weiner, 1948a, p. 78). "No communication mechanism, whether electrical or not, can call on the future to influence the past, and any contrivance which requires that, at some state, we should controvert this rule, is simply unconstructible . . . once a message has been formed, a subsequent operation on it may deprive it of some of its information, but can never augment it" (Wiener, 1948b).

What has the psychotherapist, coming in the other direction from his clinical work, to say about these statements? He can make certain comments and discuss them on the basis of his own experience: First, that the notion of "a precise message" or "a message which has been formed" is psychologically inconceivable to interpersonal communication. Second, that in contrast to mathematical "information," the amount of psychological information increases rather than decreases with increasingly intense (intrinsic) "noise." Third, that human beings, in their interpersonal communications, do seem to call successfully on the future to influence the past.

The mathematician is able to discuss "noise" and "information" from a formal, syntactic point of view in terms of entropy (Shannon & Weaver, 1949; Wiener, 1948a; Brillouin, 1950), relating them as quantities to formulations of the second law of thermodynamics. The psychologist regards noise and information semiotically from the pragmatic aspect. According to the common notion, as expressed in dictionaries, *noise* means "a disturbing or discordant sound." It is an emotional word. To say, "I hear a noise!" still means to most people, "I am disturbed." To say, "I have information!" means, "I know something." The common notion of noise usually connotes "what I don't want to hear," and of information "what I do want to hear." The mathematician, in speaking, for example, of "combating noise" and "undesirable uncertainty," seems to accept these axiological connotations (Shannon & Weaver, 1949, pp. 35, 99, 109), which the psychiatrist expresses as the anxiety aroused by noise and the feeling of security which comes from knowing something, respectively.

Since the psychiatrist is generally not equipped to deal rigorously with the mathematical concepts of "noise" and "information," it is fortunate that the mathematician sometimes indicates, implicitly and explicitly, that his discussions of these two quantities are influenced by the concepts of "desirability" and "intention." This provides a common area where the two disciplines overlap in their study of communication. If the psychiatrist defines information from the communicant's point of view as what he advertently desires and intends to communicate, and noise as what he inadvertently communicates without desiring or intending, an interesting situation arises. If we term the communicant for the moment a "machine," this may be stated as follows: Noise is the only factor which communicates operationally anything about the variable state of the machine itself. Information can communicate nothing about this except as a proposition whose verification depends upon scanning the noise. A machine which worked without noise would communicate nothing about the variations in its own state. When a message is desired about these variations, it must be derived from noise.

In interpersonal communication, such a message may be desired by the receiver. From the receiver's point of view, information can be defined as what he advertently desires and intends to receive, and noise as what he inadvertently receives without desiring or intending to receive. The reception of noise by the receiver interferes with his reception of information so that his reception is equivocal. If the receiver (in interpersonal communication) is interested in an apparently precise, formed message which the communicant desires and intends to transmit, then their definitions of noise and information coincide. But if the receiver is interested in the state of the communicant, then what is noise to the communicant becomes information to the receiver, and what is information to the communicant becomes noise to the receiver, since it interferes with his clear reception of the message he desires to receive so that his reception is equivocal. Thus in the psychological situation, what is information at one moment can become noise at the next moment, and vice versa, by a mere change of attitude on the part of the receiver. Furthermore, since the receiver can reevaluate what has already happened, what was noise in the past can become information in the future, and vice versa. The situation is somewhat analogous in the case of machines, insofar as they are objects of human observation. Although these statements are based on a shift in defining "noise" and "information" from the syntactic to the pragmatic point of view, they nevertheless present aspects to be considered in any mathematical theory of communication which takes psychological factors into account.

This position can be generalized psychologically in the following proposition: In the case of any machine which is a "black box" (the communicant), the amount of information which can be derived concerning the state of the machine itself is a direct function of the (intrinsic) noise. If the machine functions perfectly, this type of information is limited to the information that it is functioning perfectly. Specifically, a theoretically perfect diplomat reveals nothing of his inner life. The only information he communicates about himself to others is that he has perfect manners. On the other hand, the ambivalence of an ardent lover or a deadly enemy is communicated only by the noise, if any, which contaminates the precisely formed message he intends to convey. It might be possible to increase the area of mutual understanding between cybernetics and psychology by analyzing this proposition in terms of entropy in such a fashion as to make the analysis psychologically cogent. P. W. Bridgman (in Brillouin, 1949) pointed out the difficulty in dealing in terms of entropy with any system containing living organisms. This difficulty may arise *a fortiori* in the case of psychological systems; nevertheless, some psychologists have been sufficiently intrigued by the possibility to write about it (Bernfeld & Feitelberg, 1934; Penrose, 1931; Berne, 1947; Ostow, 1949).

It might appear that the problem is no more complex than dealing by communication theory with a talking movie of a person who is not acting, so that, for example, the sound track and the pictures may be regarded as noise and information respectively, or vice versa. But it is not that simple. In interpersonal communication, the message is not manifest immediately to the receiver any more than it is to the communicant; and both parties may be exerting strenuous efforts to confuse noise with information, and vice versa. Common clinical examples of these deceptive maneuvers are as follows: 1) "I'm talking a lot; therefore I'm telling you a lot." 2) "My slip of the tongue was accidental; therefore you must not judge me by it." 3) "He says he loves me; therefore he does." 4) "She forgot my birthday because she is absentminded." Whether it is possible to relate these complications to matters which the mathematician is already capable of dealing with, such as memory and coding, remains to be seen.

The Latent Communication

The position taken here that is to be justified heuristically in regard to interpersonal communication, especially in the clinical situation, is as follows: That the notion of "a precise message" is psychologically inconceivable; that the amount of potential psychological information increases rather than decreases with increasingly intense (intrinsic) noise; that the future can be successfully called upon to influence the past.

The crux of the matter from the psychological viewpoint is the differentiation between "manifest communications" and "latent communications." To illustrate this, it is convenient to consider first a communication which is indirect in time, place, and person, such as a message from antiquity.

An interesting and cogent example is the Rhind Papyrus (Newman, 1952). Thirty-six hundred years ago, an Egyptian scribe named Ahmose was attempting to communicate to some countrymen a clever method of dealing with problems in arithmetic. Reading the English translation today, one cannot help being interested in the manifest communication, which describes a fascinating but highly inefficient method of solving such problems. This method is what Ahmose desired and intended to communicate. But to the modern reader, even more interesting is what he did not advertently intend to communicate, the communication latent in his papyrus, which concerns, among other things, a certain amount of carelessness, a lack of intellectual integrity, a preponderant interest in food and how to preserve it from the ravages of mice, and an undemocratic attitude.

A prehistoric kitchen midden is an even more striking example of a latent communication, since it was not intended as a communication at all and yet communicates a great deal to future generations; e.g., dates (Kulp, et al., 1951).

With this preparation, one can approach the more subtle situation met with in the direct *vis-à-vis* communications of clinical practice. At a certain stage of his treatment, a patient bought a recording machine. He would dictate his dreams during the night and proudly bring the machine to the psychiatrist's office in the morning and run them off. This was intended to demonstrate his efficiency and cooperation, but instead showed his fear of interpersonal relationships and his hostility to the psychiatrist. He filled the machine with manifest communications which were of far less importance at the time than the latent communication signified by his purchase of the machine for this sole purpose. Furthermore, his eulogies of the machine inadvertently revealed far more about himself than they did about the recorder.

From the consideration of examples such as these, it becomes evident that the value of a communication (to the receiver) cannot be set by the communicant, but only by the receiver. No matter how anxious the communicant is to form a precise message, his communication cannot be limited to what he intends. Furthermore, the unintended communications, which from his point of view are "noise," are of more psychological value than the intended ones. But this depends on what the receiver regards as information; the patient's wife, for example, was unable at the time to see any significance in his purchase of the machine. During her own subsequent treatment, however, it happened that a great many of her husband's actions which she had previously ignored now became very informative, so that what had previously seemed like a lot of noise was transformed into information, particularly when she took the timing and the status of the communicant into account. Similarly in the case of the papyrus, the precise message which Ahmose intended is not so precise after all, and the less precise it is, the more we learn about Ahmose and his people, mainly because our distance in time from their culture enables us to be more objective. The random, disarranged, and once noisome kitchen midden also becomes very informative after the lapse of many centuries.

In the case of interpersonal relationships, in general, intended, precise, formal, rational, verbal communications are of less value than inadvertent, ambiguous, informal, nonrational, nonverbal communications; for in such cases the receiver is not interested in the information the communicant intends but in the psychological reality behind it.* "Arithmetical problems about granaries can be

---

*These are principles well known explicitly or implicitly to all psychiatrists and psychologists, and for that matter to all physicians. The probability of their validity is increased by the fact that students of other disciplines, viewing other aspects, come to similar conclusions. Among linguists, for example, E. H. Sturtevant (1947, p. 48) takes an almost cynical position: "All real intentions and emotions got themselves expressed involuntarily, and as yet nothing but intention and emotion had called for expression. So voluntary communication can scarcely have been called upon except to deceive; language must have been invented for the purpose of lying." Concerning the specificity of nonverbal communications, another linguist, Mario Pei (1949, p. 13) says: "It is further estimated that some seven hundred thousand distinct elementary gestures can be produced by facial expressions, postures, movements of the arms, wrists, fingers, etc., and their combinations." Seven hundred thousand is more than the number of words in the English language, including a few hundred thousand archaic and technical terms (ibid, p. 111).

Still, as to the relative values of verbal and nonverbal communications, there are contrasting viewpoints. Darwin (1886) says: "The movements of expression . . . serve as the first means of communication. . . . They reveal the thoughts and intentions of others more truly than do words, which may be falsified." Freud (1940, p. 84) remarks on the other hand: "Speech owes its importance to its aptitude for mutual understanding in the herd, and upon it the identification of the individuals with one another largely rests."

solved," means at the most superfiical psychological level: "I am interested in granaries"; and "I am cooperative" means *"I feel I* should tell *you* at this *time* that I am cooperative."

These observations make certain defining statements possible from the psychological point of view. Any emission of energy which affects an organism may be called a communication, providing it is understood by the receiver. For example, Mario Pei refers to "the broader definition of language" as "any transfer of meaning" (1949, p. 10). Whatever cannot be understood is not a communication. Only a person who understands the actions of bees can receive communications from them (Krogh, 1948). An image on a television screen is a communication to the public; "snow" on the screen is a communication only insofar as the receiving organism understands how television works.

A communication is *understood* when it changes the distribution of psychic cathexes in the receiving organism. Any change in the psychic cathexes in an organism, such as that brought about by a communication, changes its potentialities for action. Cathexis refers to the charge of "psychic energy" on a psychic image, and the investment of such an image with feeling and significance. Not everything which changes cathectic distribution and, hence, potentialities for action, is a communication: Metabolic changes, fantasies, and dreams may do the same thing. The *value* of a communication is the extent to which it changes quantitatively the cathectic distributions in the communicant and the receiver and, hence, their potentialities for action. The value is the quantitative aspect of the quality of being understood, and changes on a time scale. It is principally discussed here from the receiver's viewpoint. *Interpersonal* communication generally refers here to *vis-à-vis* communication which influences the development of the relationship between the autonomous portions of the personalities concerned. *Intend* (in this discussion of the latent communication) is used with its common dictionary implication of conscious design, determination, and direction.

Clinical Applications

In the case of machines, there are at least two kinds of messages received: One is the message which is put into the machine as information; another is the message which the machine sends about its own state as noise. Similarly, there are two kinds of communications between people: One refers to the manifest topic of communication, the other to the state of the communicant. The latter, as psychiatrists know, is generally latent, for if a man is asked: "How are you?" he reveals the true state of affairs, not by the manifest content of his reply, but by his manner, his choice of words, and a multitude of other clues. It has been traditionally agreed for at least five thousand years that in the development of interpersonal relationships, the state of a communicant (with regard to *Maat* or righteousness, for example) is more important than what he or she is saying. In the present terminology, the latent communication is generally of more value in this regard than the manifest communication. Its superior value is well known to the layman who remarks: "It's not what she says, it's the way she says it!"

There must be some way for the receiver to understand the latent communication. With a certain part of his ego, the communicant tries "to form a precise message." But what comes out is a configuration to which many functions make their contributions and through which they potentially reveal themselves. The receiver understands as much of this as he is ready to, but it seems always more than the communicant advertently intended. Just as the communicant communicates, so the receiver perceives through a configuration of many functions. What is important is that he understands more than he is aware of, just as the communicant reveals more than he is aware of. What he understands but is not aware of is his "latent response" to the communication. He may or may not eventually become fully aware of all that he understands, but his psychic cathexes are redistributed and his potentialities for action changed much more than he is aware of at a given moment. The following case demonstrates the nature of the latent response and that it is on the basis of the latent response that the receiver relies on the future to rearrange the past into new components of noise and information. It also shows how in the mind, information does not "exist"; it "becomes."

A man who was courting a widow tried to curry her favor by lavishing attention on her children and her dog. He frequently stated with apparent sincerity, "I love children and dogs." The widow's manifest response was to think, speak, and act with conscious intent as though she accepted his manifest communication at face value. But along with the latter she received an impression which was not yet a manifest response. She noticed that his voice had a peculiar tone when he made this declaration. This tone was "noise" in many senses of the word. It was not intended, it communicated no information about his love (at the time), it was a vibration of the "machine" which made his words less clear, and it was disturbing. On one occasion, she observed him (without his knowledge) snarling at a child, and on another occasion kicking a dog. On each of these occasions an interesting event took place: A lot of "noises," of whose value and import the widow was not previously aware and which she had never intended to notice, were suddenly integrated so that her attention was adverted to them and they became informative: "He was lying *all along* when he said he loved children and dogs." The wooer's manifest communication had carried with it some latent communications. These activated in the widow a fund of inadvertent latent responses which led to her feeling of uneasiness. When his insincerity became manifest, her stored-up latent responses became manifest to her. While they were still latent, however, they were understood in the sense that they changed her potentialities for action so that, without precisely knowing why or consciously planning to, she maintained a certain reserve and spied upon him a little.

This example attempts to demonstrate why certain responses are called "latent" and why such latent influences are called "responses." The distinction between latent responses and latent content must now be discussed. A young scientist was greatly interested in the very subject discussed here: the relationship between cybernetics and psychology. He maintained that his ideas on the subject were objective, and on the surface they appeared so, but it soon became evident that he was not aware of a response of his to the problem. He became very defensive when the inclusion in his discussion of a certain quotation was questioned, a remark of O'Brien's in Orwell's *1984:* "Do you suppose our mathematicians are unequal to that?" It soon appeared that the literature he had read on communication theory had made him uneasy, so that quite unconsciously he had developed a hostile attitude, for he feared that further progress in the subject would reduce the esthetic values in human society. His latent response to the manifest and latent communications of the mathematicians was highly charged with resentment toward them. But the latent content of his hostility referred to something far in the past: his fear that his very conscientious ("mathematical") father would deprive him of the pleasure of having romantic ("esthetic") fantasies about his mother. He had a latent response (which became manifest in analysis) about the mathematicians, based on latent content about himself.

A woman reported: "I dreamed about a kitten." Both her latent communication, and the latent response in the analyst's mind were, as they both discovered later, something about a miscarriage, although at the time they talked about cats. The latent content in her mind, which determined her latent communication, was about herself, and the analyst's latent response was also about her and not about himself. In general, latent content refers to the latent perception of what concerns the individual's own psychology; latent response refers to the latent perception through communication of someone else's psychology, or, more broadly, to the latent perception through communication of something about external reality. Doubtful cases are taken care of in a formal way by defining communication as an understood emission of energy which affects the organism. The psychiatrist's latent response in clinical communication is usually a response to: the patient's latent response to a previous communication, plus the patient's latent content. For example: "This patient doesn't know that he is angry at what I said, which reminds him of earlier experiences; is that why I'm being unusually careful of what I say?" And conversely for the patient sometimes, *mutatis mutandis*. For example: "The doctor doesn't know that he is responding to my provocation because of his earlier experiences; is that what I have to settle with him?"*

---

*The latent response may be represented by, but is not identical with, a preconscious stream of associations in the mind of the receiver. This stream of thoughts can sometimes be detected by introspection

The concept of the latent response may now be recognized as having some familiar connotations. In clinical practice it refers to the latent communication of the subconscious reactions of the patient to his situation and to the subconscious perception of these reactions by the analyst, ideally without any interference from his own anxieties. In other words, it applies in this situation mainly to the perception of the transference reactions with a minimum of interference from countertransference or anxiety, excluding what the analyst is able to verbalize to himself immediately. The peculiar skill of the analyst in this respect is to be able to detect more than is ordinarily detected of the latent communication. This skill comes through training in detecting his own latent responses and in purifying them by segregating the latent thoughts caused by countertransference and anxiety. This is not meant to imply that there is necessarily a one-to-one relationship between a manifest communication and a manifest response, or between a latent communication and a latent response, although there is an empirical relationship.

Another familiar aspect of the latent response is its relationship to the unconscious or preconscious perceptive ego; that is, to intuition. In other words, the latent response to a communication is the intuitive knowledge of

---

while listening. It may be more or less influenced by the latent content which the communication activates in the receiver and is usually a compromise formation of the two influences: the latent response and the latent content which the manifest and latent communications activate. Patients often seem to respond to this stream of associations, when it occurs, rather than to the manifest communications of the analyst. T. Reik (1949, chaps. 17 & 18) offers some good examples of this preconscious phenomenon. He also describes excellently some latent responses, though not by that name (1949, chaps. 16 & 17). All this is difficult to state more simply because of the multiplicity of vectors.

the receiver. . . . He may not even know what it is that he knows, but he behaves or reacts in a specific way as if his actions or reactions were based on some special knowledge.* In fact, he may not even know that he knows something, yet behaves as if he did.

The receiver may not be aware that anything has been communicated besides the manifest content; or, if he is, he may not know how the latent communication is conveyed. Nevertheless, the distribution of his psychic cathexes is changed so that he behaves or reacts as if he had some additional understanding.

It is interesting to note that, in general, women seem to be more aware of, and to place more value consciously on the latent communication than men. For example, they are more apt to be aware of being influenced to a greater degree by a man's mood, zeal, or tone of voice than by what he says. Many men prefer to think that they are primarily influenced by the manifest communication.

Summary

Psychological aspects of the mathematical concepts of "noise" and "information" are discussed. Although these concepts are now mathematically related to the second law of thermodynamics, their evaluation still involves psychological problems. The most important point in this respect is that it is "noise" and not "information" which

---

*This is reminiscent of Schilder's statement regarding dogs: "It is also true that the sound which for the dog has become a promise that feeding will occur is no longer like any other sound. It has gone through many more constructive processes. For the dog the sound has the import of feeding" (1942, p. 259). Schilder epitomizes the situation when he speaks of the prior wordless state that every thought goes through before it is formulated (in Fenichel, 1945, p. 46).

signals the state of the machine itself. This introduces an apparent paradox in the study of communication when "noise" and "information" are defined from a psychological point of view.

An attempt is made to justify heuristically some important differences in communication theory between the mathematical (syntactic) and the psychological (pragmatic) points of view. The psychologist differs from the mathematician in considering: 1) that the notion of "a precise message" is psychologically inconceivable; 2) that the amount of potential psychological information increases rather than decreases with increasingly intense (intrinsic) noise; 3) that the future can be successfully called upon to influence the past.

In interpersonal communications, "noise" is of more value than "information," since in such cases it is of more value to the communicants to know about each other's states than to give "information" to each other. "Noise" carries latent communications from the communicant. Manifest and latent communications arouse latent responses in the receiver which are important to both parties and are of special interest to psychiatrists.

4 Primal Images and Primal Judgment

A PRIMAL IMAGE is the image of an infantile object relationship; that is, of the use of the function of an erogenous zone for social expression. A primal judgment is the understanding (correct or incorrect) of the potentialities of the object relationship represented by the image. In the normal adult, under ordinary conditions, neither the primal image nor the primal judgment comes into awareness. Instead, a more or less distant derivative, which is called here an intuition, may become conscious.

Primal images are presymbolic representations of interpersonal transactions, whose study leads directly into certain important areas of psychopathology. These images, which have a special quality reminiscent of eidetic images, may be regarded as clear and indirect representations of the psychophysiological bases of another person's social expression. Primal judgments imply an understanding, based on such images, of certain archaic unconscious attitudes of other people. These attitudes are derived from early instinctual vicissitudes and express a deep and persistent infantile quality in object relationships. Such "primal" understandings may be selectively influenced by the percipient's own archaic needs and strivings but,

Copyright 1955, *The Psychiatric Quarterly* (29, 634-658), by whom this reprint was permitted. (Originally entitled, "Intuition IV: Primal Images and Primal Judgment.")

nevertheless, appear to reflect accurately in many cases something in another person's mode of relating. As the exposition will necessarily be complex, a clinical example may be given at the outset so that the reader will have a notion of what is being talked about.

Belle, a 40-year-old housewife, gradually became aware that her relationships with men were somewhat stereotyped. There were some whom she mocked in a more or less subtle way, while she tormented others. In the course of time, she sensed that her mockery was the tincture of a feeling of relief, while the cloak of the tormentor concealed a sense of danger. One day she recounted with a jeering feeling of laughter a conversation with a known exhibitionist. How droll he would look, she thought, taking off his clothes to exhibit his flaccid penis! This was her conception of exhibitionism. It brought to mind her thoughts about the therapist, who was such a flaccid sort of man that he reminded her of her dear old grandmother. But he did not always appear so. Sometimes he reminded her of her husband, a man as implacable as stone, whose tremendous erections frightened her and whom she teased cruelly, leading him on sexually until he could hardly contain his passion, and then at the last moment freezing him out with ruthless frigidity. Only the other day she had glanced at the therapist and thought she could see the conformation of his genitals, and had tried to determine if his penis was flabby or erect. She used to do the same thing with her father, when she played on his lap as a child.

The men she jeered at did have a flaccid quality, she saw now, and it was the virile ones she tormented. External evidence seemed to confirm her judgments of some of the men she encountered. She began to feel that such judgments, which had previously been unconscious, were based on an image of each man's penis, which had also previously been unconscious. Indeed, it turned out later that she had been as a child (and still was to some extent) obsessed by sexual images. The penis image reminded her of her husband when he took a sunbath. Sometimes he would have an erection, and she could not bear the sight. Once he told her a joke about an erection, which was so graphic that she could not tolerate the image it conjured up, and she became nauseated. "I could see that fellow's penis right in front of me—hairy, ugly, and raw." She could talk of the vagina in an intellectual way but could not bear to think of it as she really pictured it, "a raw red slimy gash." The image terrified her, and she desperately avoided it. "My images are too clear. It frightens me. I just can't bear to think of it." Smell seemed to play a prominent part in this type of imagery with her, as it does in many cases.

It will be noted that she reacted to her "too clear" images as though the organs pictured had special potentialities for her. It is such images that the writer proposes to call primal images, and such judgments as she made of people, based on these images—"This man is flaccid (in his potentialities toward me)" and "This man is virile (in his potentialities toward me)"—that the writer would term primal judgments.

Among the earliest psychological phenomena discussed by Freud, in connection with one of his very first analytic cases, Mrs. Emmy von N., (Freud & Breuer, 1937), he refers almost in passing to "plastic images." This is a topic which he did not systematically follow up, although he repeatedly mentions it in connection with dreams and wit. These images, as they occur in hysterics such as Belle, seem to be closely related to, or identical with, primal images. If so, then they are also closely related to Jaensch's eidetic images (1930), which seem to have many of the descriptive qualities discernible in primal imagery.

The qualities common to both eidetic images and primal images, and which differentiate them from ordinary memory images, are: a pseudoperceptual quality; superior clearness, richness, and accuracy of detail; and more brilliant coloration. All these are present even when the period of exposure is shorter than that usually required for a vivid memory image. Although they are both "images of hallucinatory clearness," they can be distinguished from hallucinations and pseudo-hallucinations. Eidetic images, like primal images, are supposed to exist in other sense fields besides the visual; it is even said that ordinary "images" do not exist at all in the field of the lower senses, and that there all past sensory experiences are revived eidetically.

Jaensch, however, does not seem to emphasize clearly the dynamic effects of special imagery in influencing interpersonal relationships. This is the purpose of the present communication. It is pertinent, however, that Fenichel does remark that "eidetic types may be designated as perception fixations" (1945, p. 53). Silberer's "functional phenomenon" (1951) appears to be a symbolic derivative rather than the directed expression of the "primal" phenomena dealt with here. Two recent rather comprehensive symposia on perception and personality (Rapaport, 1951; Hunt, 1944) fail to note this particular kind of dynamic imagery. A recent article by Smythies (1953) borders on the subject, but the nearest thing to a systematic psychodynamic discussion is Ferenczi's paper "On Obscene Words" (1916). Several disjointed sentences from that work may be quoted as an introduction to the discussion.

"An obscene word has a peculiar power of compelling the hearer to imagine the object it denotes, the sexual organ or function, in *substantial actuality*. . . . These words as such possess the capacity of compelling the hearer to revive memory pictures in a regressive and hallucinatory manner. . . . The obscene verbal images retain as does all repressed material the characters of a more primitive type of imagination." Ferenczi speaks of "a high degree of regressive tendency," a vivid "mimicry of imagery," and of "primitive" attributes.

Ferenczi is talking of the evocation of such images by the stimulus of an obscene word, while the concern here is with their spontaneous activation during the course of an interpersonal relationship. Ferenczi's work has recently been reconsidered and enlarged upon, primarily from the linguistic point of view, by Stone (1954), who gives a large number of references, including Bergler's paper of 1936; but again the viewpoint is not directly concerned with the present problem. Kestenberg (1953) also discusses primitive sensory experience, with references to the literature. But so far as the writer knows, no one has yet systematically discussed the connection of such images with judgments of, and subsequent reactions to, the people in the environment; that is, essentially, their relationship to intuitive processes. Perhaps Jung (1946), in a nondynamic way, comes closest, especially when speaking of "primordial images."

What will be considered here are the following topics: 1) The infantile origins of primal judgments. 2) The pathogenicity of primal images. 3) The relationship of primal images and primal judgments to intuitive processes.

But first it is desirable to try to clarify some of the terminology which will be employed. The following definitions are taken from some of the writer's preliminary communications on the subject.

Preliminary Considerations

Every human being is capable of making judgments by the use of functions whose processes are not ordinarily verbalized. In practice, judgments of reality are probably made through the integration of a series of types of cognitive processes. It appears that the most important and influential judgments which human beings make concerning each other are the products of preverbal processes—cognition without insight—which function almost automatically below the level of consciousness. . . . To go a step further . . . [the individual] may not only be unaware how he made a certain judgment and what the judgment is but he may be unaware that he has made a judgment at all. The latter is likely to be the situation in what are here called "primal judgments."

By *judgment* is meant an image of reality which affects behavior and feelings toward reality. An *image* is formed by integrating sensory and other impressions with each other and with inner tensions based on present needs and past experiences. By *reality* is meant the potentialities for interaction of all the energy systems in the universe; this implies the past. A judgment concerning one person, the *agent* (corresponding to the communicant), by another, the *percipient* (corresponding to the receiver), is here called a *diagnosis*. Diagnoses are made through the medium of communication. Any transfer of energy from without to within an organism may be called a *communication*, provided it is understood by the receiver. A communication is *understood* when it changes the distribution of the psychic cathexes in the receiving organism. Any change in the psychic cathexes in an organism, such as that brought about by a communication, changes its potentialities for action. *Cathexis* refers to the charge of energy on a psychic image, and the investment of such an image with feeling and significance.

An *interpersonal* communication is any communication, through any modality of energy, between two people. A *manifest* interpersonal communication corresponds to the successfully executed conscious intent of the agent, while a *latent* communication is inadvertent. In general, the interpersonal communications considered here are *direct* in time, place, and person, that is, *vis-à-vis*.

An intuition is a special kind of diagnosis resulting from archaic processes which are subconscious (that is, preconscious and/or unconscious). Intuitions, as consciously perceived, are derivatives of primal judgments, which are based on primal images activated by latent communications. "Primal" is used in the Freudian sense, as in "primal fantasy" and "primal scene." In fact, it is probable that many primal images are based on primal scene memories. The word carries with it connotations of the archaic infantile psychological process, and, indeed, the question at issue here might be most succinctly exemplified by the query: "How does an infant make a diagnosis and what are his diagnostic categories?"

Infancy and Childhood

Fenichel describes the perceptions of infants as follows: "The first images are large in extent, all enveloping and inexact. They do not consist of elements that are later put together, but rather of units, wholes, which only later are recognized as containing different elements . . . the perceptions of many sense organs overlap. The more primitive senses, especially the kinesthetic sensations and the data of depth sensibility prevail . . . the contents that are perceived are also different. Hermann called perceptions 'which the small child possesses, but which later disappear for inner or external reasons,' primal perceptions

. . . To a greater part the characteristics of archaic perception result from its 'unobjective' character, its emotional nature. The world is perceived according to the instincts as a possible source of satisfaction or as a possible threat . . . the primitive experiences are felt as still undifferentiated wholes which make their appearance repeatedly" (1945, p. 38 f.). He also states that "the pleasure principle is incompatible with correct judgment."

Such ideas concerning the nature of imagery in young children can only be inferential, but it is probable that no adult ever sees anyone as glorious or as evil as his mother appeared to him during his first years, or as splendid or as terrifying as his father, except in states of sleep, intoxication, ecstasy, or psychosis. It is likely that some of the images of infants are enormously cathected and have an uncanny magical immediacy and urgency which the normal adult never experiences (cf. R. Spitz). The representations which the normal adult may unearth are the shadows of these archaic ones, with the primal cathexes long ago diluted and withdrawn to be distributed among derivatives.

It is safe to infer from the available evidence that the infant's diagnostic categories are based on various aspects of self-interest. It is probable, furthermore, that his diagnoses are based on latent communications and not on manifest ones. The "friendly" smile which is not sincere may give way under his ruthless appraisal. He often appears to react to the hidden insincerity rather than to the manifested smile. But there are frequent exceptions. For example, his reputed skill in detecting latent communications can be beguiled by an appeal to his immediate needs, which may be the sort of thing that disturbs the compatibility of the pleasure principle with correct judgments.

The infant, as he is observed in his relationships with

adults, seems adept at divining what lies behind any but the most stable defenses and derivatives. As he grows up, he learns to civilize these primal judgments and fit them into a cultural framework, and his putative awareness of just what he thinks people want from him or are likely to do to him becomes obscured.

Originally, he must see people in a primitive way, relating his observations primarily to himself as an organism whose function is to survive and get direct satisfaction from his environment. Insofar as his diagnostic capabilities are learned, we may suppose that he watches the expressions of the people around him when they are disposed toward him in various ways, and learns by some kind of experience what various emotional expressions signify for his own future. Thus he becomes a judge of other people, such as strangers. His judgment is sufficiently refined even during the first year so that he can distinguish between people who want to hurt him and people who have to hurt him even though they do not wish to. For example, he knows that the doctor is going to hurt him even before he sees the needle, but he quickly forgives the doctor after it is over. On the other hand, he bursts into unforgiving tears when he sees the mean little boy approaching.

An infant under six months who was brought to the clinic by his mother responded happily to one social worker's cooing, but burst into tears and buried his face in his mother's breast when another tried similar tactics. He responded in the same way on subsequent visits. The child's "diagnosis" happened to correspond to the impressions of those who knew the social workers well. The first worker was known for the affectionate relationship which existed between herself and her own children, while the second was a spinster whose outward appearance was agreeable enough but who was felt by the staff to be unconsciously hostile to mothers and to infants. It is noteworthy in this connection that some people seem to quaver beneath the appraising stare of a babe in arms, just as many do under the diagnostic regard of the unpredictable, "foolproof," and uncontrollable psychiatrist, as if they feared in both cases that their defenses and maneuvers would not avail to conceal their own primal, exploiting needs.

It may be inferred that an infant's responses to people, especially strangers, such as baby-sitters, are based on primal judgments appropriate to his age, as to whether they threaten his security or promise satisfaction for his current needs: in the oral phase, for example, "Does this one bring me what I crave?" The schizophrenic's judgments often have a similar infantile flavor; this is known in one way or another to many skillful therapists, who guide their behavior in the treatment accordingly.

Schizophrenia

A hebephrenic was able to talk about his primal images in some detail. He was observed on the ward laughing and muttering to himself, completely out of touch with his surroundings. The following day, however, he had a rather complete remission and was able to discuss his thoughts coherently. The psychiatrist, who thought he knew what was troubling the patient, inquired:

"What you saw was intolerable, wasn't it?"

Patient: "Yes, it was awful. I couldn't bear it."

Therapist: "It was too close."

Patient: "Yes, right in front of me."

Therapist: "What was it?"

Patient: "A woman's legs around my head, and her vagina right up against my mouth."

Therapist: "Did you know who it was?"
Patient: "Yes."
The therapist thought it wise not to press the point further. His intuition concerning the patient's primal image about cunnilinctus had turned out to be correct, and he did not think it advisable to risk disturbing the patient in order to confirm his surmise as to the identity of the woman. The patient stated that this was an image, and not a vision, and that there had been two other forms of the same representation: "a scale model in the corner of the room, a man and a woman having intercourse and doing that, like a photograph," and that he "also saw it in my mind sometimes, just an image of a man and woman doing that." But as for what had made him smile the day before, "It was those legs being right there, right in my face."

In this case, the patient visualized his relationship to an important woman in terms of the juxtaposition of selected erogenous zones, and this image was so absorbing that he was oblivious of his surroundings. Such an image may be regarded as expressing some archaic social concept.

It has already been mentioned that smell imagery is characteristic of primal images. So is taste, or at any rate, intraoral sensations. A "borderline" schizophrenic remarked: "I looked at the woman standing there talking and I could imagine her breasts with brown nipples and a little hair around them. Ugh! I can taste hair in my mouth already. Pooh!" (Sharpe, 1950, discusses the significance of such words as *ugh* and *pooh*.)

The same borderline individual gave a good example of how primal imagery affected his judgment of people. "When that woman came into the room, I thought she was pretty, but somehow I knew that her vagina would be dry and ugly. How could such a pretty woman have such an ugly vagina?" He acted not on his superficial judgment of her prettiness but on his primal image of her genitals, and avoided her.

A comparison of these two cases helps to differentiate the psychotic from the borderline case. The second man was carrying on his business and his home life. It is evident enough that if the image of the hairy nipple right in his mouth became too insistent, he would no longer be able to function in everyday life. If his "vaginal diagnoses," that is, his primal images of the vaginas of the women he met, got out of hand, he would be unable to venture into society. In the fully psychotic hebephrenic case, the images appeared in consciousness in their full primality, fully cathected. It was, at least in part, the delicately balanced repression of full primality and full cathexis which enabled the other man to carry on in a "borderline" state.

Thus certain well-known accompaniments of schizophrenia can be accounted for in some cases by the assumption that primal images break through into consciousness with such an uncontrollably strong cathexis as to interfere with normal mental functioning. This may help to explain the widely credited "keen intuition" of some schizophrenics; they are in an excellent position to make primal judgments, since their primal images are in full flower. A lack of affect about ordinary events may be accounted for by the fact that much of the available cathexis is taken up by primal images. Autistic emotional mimicry may be a response to those images. Hallucinations might be regarded from this particular point of view as an extrajection of primal images in order to "leave some room in the mind" to get out from under them and allow for the reassuring illusion of autonomy.

The decisive effect which primal images and primal judgments may have in determining the behavior and destiny of a schizophrenic is demonstrated by the following example. A young woman was transferred to an inexperienced psychiatrist after she had been greatly relieved of many symptoms of schizophrenia. She asked the new therapist a myriad of questions, some of which he answered in a straightforward manner. She replied on a subsequent visit with a fantasy that he was giving her intense sexual pleasure by administering an enema. Her own diagnostic problem seemed to be summarized by the question: "Is he or is he not the kind of man who would stimulate my anus in a certain way?" Thus the therapist had submitted to a psychological test which she administered in a covert way with great skill and subtlety. The score came in the form of a fantasy concerning an enema. This fantasy decided her future relationship with him, and represented a primal judgment with almost no disguise. It was not long before she sought treatment elsewhere.

The patient well exemplifies Fenichel's statement that "primitive symbolism is a part of the way in which conceptions are formed in prelogical thinking: comprehension of the world radiates from instinctual demands and fears, so that the first objects are possible means of gratification or possible threats; the first ideas are . . . wholes comprehended in a still undifferentiated way, united by the emotional responses they have provoked" (1945, p. 49).

In normal adults, primal images rarely come into awareness, and primal judgments are filtered through a heavy layer of cultural determinants so that they emerge in a civilized form; even if a well-integrated man does express a primal judgment, such as "So-and-so is a big prick!" or "He's a sucker!" he is seldom aware of what he really means, or of the image upon which his judgment is based. With some schizophrenics, however, this verbal, culturally determined interpretation of archaic latent responses or perceptions is broken down; such an individual becomes uncultured, like an infant. He refuses to accept people's presentations of themselves and, instead, makes direct, uncivilized primal judgments. This, along with his other problems in dealing with people, makes it difficult for him to function in society. If he goes to a gathering and has an urgent feeling that one person would like to stimulate his anus and another wants him to perform cunnilinctus, he may behave in a very bizarre, unpredictable, and infantile fashion because he has too many highly cathected primal images.

Neurosis

The case of Belle, like that of Emmy von N., illustrates the occurrence of primal images in neurosis. Freud and Breuer (1937) said that the hysteric suffers mostly from reminiscences. It may now be said that the reminiscences may take the form of primal images and that the "content" which is repressed may consist of a complex of ideas and feelings embodied in a highly cathected set of such images.

Among neurotics, many dreams express the primal judgment of the patient concerning the therapist. By inference from some remarks of Gitelson (1952) this might indicate at times a too-active countertransference. Primal judgments, being derived from memory traces of actual archaic experience, include many details of the behavioral situation: aim and object (Freud), and zone and mode (Erikson, 1950). Often, primal images seem to have the special quality of filling the mind. A young male patient recounted the persistence of a masturbatory fantasy involving a photograph. This image was very different from anything he had previously experienced. It seemed to fill his whole mind so that there was no room for anything else when it was "in charge." "It was so large that I could not master it." By the second evening he had succeeded in mastering it, and he felt once more in control of his mind. When it forced itself on his attention, it was almost life-size. It was so big that when he could see only part of the buttocks, he felt that his mind was full. The "mastering" resulted in his seeing it as a photograph once more in its actual size, an image which he could control, just as he could control the actual photograph. This patient was not unusually obsessional, and this was a special experience in his life.

Everyday Life

Primal judgments give rise to part of the emotional substance of everyday life. This is most apparent in the encounters with strangers. New acquaintances may be characterized in vulgar gossip as pricks, jerks, assholes, farts, stinkers, shits, suckers, or bitches, sluts, pushovers, cock teasers, cats, bleeding hearts, clotheshorses. All these opprobrious terms are intuitive derivatives of primal images. The images themselves can easily be elicited by free association to any of these epithets. In polite circles, a second or third derivative of the primal image is used instead of a first derivative. Even the commonplace metaphors of ordinary speech have been reduced by Sharpe (1950) to their primal elements; that is, their roots in archaic experience.

The significant thing is that all these social judgments are made through latent communications. The sucker does not have to be observed sucking anybody before the judgment can be made, the stinker does not have to have a bad odor, nor does the cat need to be seen scratching her rival. In fact, the sucker may go out of his way to appear like a prick, and the slut may try to disguise herself as a clotheshorse, but, in both cases, a perceptive observer can easily see behind the mask.

Furthermore, this is the stuff that long-term relationships are made of. The clotheshorse and the sucker, the bleeding heart and the jerk, the slut and the shit, somehow know how to find each other, and often fall in love with each other at first sight, or so they say.

The rapidity with which primal judgments are made in everyday life is illustrated not only by cases where people fall in love at first sight, or fall in hate at first sight, perhaps "hating each other's guts," but even by more commonplace occurrences. An individual of either sex may merely observe a strange man walking down the street and be impelled to remark: "I'd sure hate to meet him in a dark alley!" The tremendous connotations of the word "slut" may be brought into play after a single glance at a strange woman, dooming her, as it were, to a whole life of misery in the blink of an eye. The sinister fantasies about the dark alley and the messy image of the soiled woman do not have to be brought into consciousness on such occasions for judgments to be made. But a young man in a public lavatory listened to three or four of the abstracted, narcissistic, petulant sniffles of the slouching man at the next urinal and immediately saw with the keenest imagery the autistic murderous sexual cruelty which this man's attitude brought to his mind. The impression was so vivid that he remembered it for years afterward. This demonstrates the spontaneity and rapidity and power with which primal images (correct or incorrect) can be activated.

The psychology of these images may be clarified as follows. Many (or perhaps all) individuals have a store of primal images which seem on the available evidence to be derived from childhood experiences and fantasies and which are selectively activated in response to the behavior of people they encounter. The primal judgment is embedded in, and emerges from, its pictorial representation in the image. In the normal adult, in the usual course of events, the residual cathexis is weak enough so that the activated images are not difficult to keep under control, and only relatively distant, verbal, well-integrated, culturally determined derivatives come into awareness as intuitions. In polite society, the derivatives are more distant and often more verbose and formal than in less cultivated circles. It may take a lot of words to say "jerk" in polite language. In the neurotic, because of the traumatic nature of the experiences upon which the images are based, the cathexis is difficult to master, and the activated images arouse great anxiety, as in the case of Belle. If the mastery is only partial, the image threatens to break through, and special psychic mechanisms must be brought into play for the emergency. In borderline cases, the images themselves come into awareness but the cathexis is separately dealt with by some psychic mechanism such as repression or displacement, so that primal judgments are made but do not have pathological force and immediacy in modifying the individual's behavior.

In some schizophrenics, the mastery mechanisms break down and the activated primal images may come into awareness with their full, pathologically strong cathexis, bringing with them direct primal judgments of considerable force and urgency. The attention of such a patient may be diverted from his other interests into a struggle with these archaic phenomena. If they threaten to overwhelm him, he may save himself eventually by extrajecting the pathologically cathected images in a camouflaged form as auditory or visual hallucinations, thus reducing the intensity of his struggle. Hallucination is then the price he must pay for the mercy of camouflage. This does not "explain" hallucinations, but it may account for certain features of some hallucinations.

Experiments with Intuition

The experimental study of intuitive processes [previously described] brought to light some interesting inconsistencies. In . . . [the] attempt . . . to guess by inspection the civilian occupations of a large number of soldiers . . . it became apparent that what the intuitive function really perceived was "attitude toward an imponderable reality situation." The intuiter's ego then translated these perceptions into a judgment concerning occupational group.

In . . . the attempt . . . to predict by inspection the replies . . . to the . . . two questions:

1. Are you nervous?
2. Have you ever been to a psychiatrist?

. . . it was noted after careful consideration of the experience: The subconscious process does not really make a diagnosis in the medical sense. It makes a preverbal judgment of the configuration, knowing nothing of diagnostic terminology. What happens is that this judgment is verbalized in diagnostic terminology. It appears that verbalizing knowledge is different from knowing about something. Much of the scanning of configurations is conditioned by early experiences, so that different individuals integrate different constellations of qualities and potentialities in observing the people they meet.

If all this is true, and it seems to be confirmed by further experience, then the normal adult, like the infant, understands some fundamental—that is, dynamically predominant—aspects of each person he meets. The infant has an immediate direct response, which is inferred to be based on self-interest. The adult, however, filters this fundamental understanding, which is a latent response, through an ego which has been heavily conditioned over a long period in a complex way, so that what the adult becomes aware of is a sorted and distorted impression, whose configuration, further, he schematizes by the process of verbalization. When one adds to the complexities introduced by the ego, those introduced by the superego and its derivatives in the normal adult, it is apparent why it is difficult for him to find his way back to the original direct response, the primal judgment. Just as the figure of the primal mother lies buried under the years—her ghost infused into the figure of his wife or some idealized or repudiated woman—so the figure of each primal judgment lies buried under his fantasies, his thoughts, and his words on each encounter with a new person.

Experiments with Primal Judgment

In the course of some studies on the possibility of isolating and controlling specific factors in group psychotherapy, the writer instituted an experiment in primal judgment. Because of his belief regarding the potential pathogenicity of primal images—a belief derived from clinical experience and supported by the spontaneous comments of colleagues—this experiment was carried out in the most prudent possible circumstances. The group consisted at that time of five individuals: Art, Belle, Carl, Jane, and May. All of them had had at least a year of group psychotherapy, and all except May had had at least two years of previous individual psychotherapy. All except Jane were having at least one individual interview between the weekly group sessions, so that their reactions to the group proceedings could be observed, and any excessive anxiety brought to the attention of the therapist. (Jane was being seen individually once every two weeks.) May was included in this particular group, because she had manifested considerable ego strength in a less advanced group.

At one session, Jane offered a good example of spontaneous primal judgment. The group members were discussing their marital relationships, and Carl asked a question which was considered indiscreet even in that sophisticated company.

> Jane: "If Art asked me that, I'd tell him to kiss my ass. I wouldn't tell you that because you'd just tell me to go to hell. But if I told Art to do it, he would. You've got me scared, but I know I could handle him."
>
> Carl: "I sure would."
>
> Art: "You know, I've always been afraid of you, Jane. I think you've got me spotted."

This situation was complicated and revealing, because Art's oral needs were predominant in the group; and Jane later had a dream in which she wore a brassiere on her buttocks; while Carl enjoyed fighting physically with women, although he had concealed that from the group in his manifest communications. Evidently, they all sensed a good deal about each other in these primitive terms. The pertinent point was Jane's clear perception of Art's suctorial tendencies, which he himself was not fully aware of and which he had concealed from the group in his verbal participation, and her simultaneous perception of Carl's concealed sadistic tendencies. Jane demonstrated on numerous occasions her ability to make primal judgments, even against the strenuous denials and defensive concealments of the individuals concerned.

Carl was absent at a later session when Belle described how she had walked across a wooden bridge and felt an obsessive fear that she would be "sucked into the water" through the knothole. The other three members of the group by this time were able to state their free associations.

May: "She's afraid of being sucked into the rectum." One of May's statements of her own problem was that she always had to keep her rectal sphincter tightly closed.

Jane: "She's afraid of being sucked back into the vagina." Later Jane described how she felt she had to suck all her husband's semen away with her vagina during intercourse.

Art: "She's afraid she'll be sucked into something like a mouth."

In this example, each primal image and primal judgment was influenced by the percipient's own problems.

But on other occasions, their primal images coincided and seemed to be evoked by the agent's communications, without apparent contamination from the percipient's own instinctual orientation.

May: "I've always been afraid to sit close to a strange man for fear that he might vomit on me."

The other three seemed in unanimous agreement that what she was really afraid of was an ejaculation.

Belle: "I've been concerned about mineral jelly lately. First I dreamed I was a little girl and had it on my hands, then I had another dream and had it on my mouth. I asked my mother about it and she said I had it on both for sores when I was little."

Jane: "My first thought was it was on that rectal

tube you once told us about."

Art: "That's what came to my mind, too."

May did not know about Belle's childhood enemas and said nothing. Here it is significant that the "phallic" woman and the "oral" man both thought of Belle's concern in anal terms. Judging from her private interviews, it seemed that the lubricant on the rectal tube during her daily childhood enemas must have more significance to Belle than jelly on her mouth or hands in childhood.

This experiment demonstrated that under certain conditions some people can be trained to become aware of their primal images and primal judgments, both contaminated and uncontaminated. The desirable and undesirable effects of such an experiment are not pertinent to the present discussion. It did lay bare certain sources of confusion in the personal relationships of these patients and was particularly adapted to demonstrating distortions in their body images: in the examples given, the posterior breasts, and the rectum as the primary suctorial organ.

Clinical Diagnosis

The psychiatrist's position in these archaic matters is of course quite different from the patient's. The patient makes his primal judgment as part of his neurotic or psychotic processes. The schizophrenic woman referred to in the foregoing had an intense conflict about whether she wanted a man to give her an enema. Her social faculties were oriented toward determining whether a given man would be likely to do this, or, more precisely, how strongly each man was unconsciously oriented in this direction and how much his orientation coincided with her delicately balanced needs. Her primal judgment, which was very frankly expressed in her fantasies, then determined her attitude and the development of her relationship with each man. The patient's primal concern was relatively constant, in accordance with her own individuality and history, and was a matter of specific need, fear, conflict, defense, and surrender.

But the psychiatrist cannot regard his patients, as they do him, as objects for the solution of infantile conflicts and instruments for the satisfaction of his neurotic desires. The patient looks for a restricted series of latent communications from the psychiatrist: concerning the psychiatrist's virility, or his possibilities as an enema giver, or as a source of nourishment. The patient wants to know, schematically speaking, how much of some one thing the psychiatrist is. He is looking for what he needs and fears; he is a victim of the repetition-compulsion. This is exactly what the psychiatrist must not be. He does not similarly scan the patient's communications for messages related to a predetermined field (except when this is technically correct). He scans the communications to find what latent topic is most important to the patient. Particularly in the initial interview, he listens to ascertain what the patient fears or expects from him, not to discover whether he can get what he wants from the patient. He decides that the patient wants to eat him, urinate on him, poke him, or perform some similar infantile operation. He makes a primal judgment of the patient, based, not on his own restricted needs of the moment, but on what predominates in the patient's latent communications.

In the experiments on intuition ... previously [described], some observations were made regarding the particular sets of muscles which appeared to be sources of information regarding corresponding facets of the soldiers' personalities. In the first series, it was noted that the agent's attitude toward an imponderable reality situation was usually gauged primarily from clues supplied by the eyes and periocular muscles, while impressions concerning the instincts and their vicissitudes were largely based on "subconscious observation" of the muscles of the lower face, especially of those about the mouth. Head posture and mannerisms based on the tonus of the neck muscles can also be important indicators in this respect. The eyes seemed to be principally instruments of the ego, while the mouth was more expressive of functions of the id. In the second experiment, the diagnoses were based on a variety of motor activities, including voice, eye movements, and movements of the extremities. They were also influenced by an undefinable impression that normal soldiers had "nothing to hide," in contrast to neurotic soldiers on the hospital wards, who in retrospect began to seem "as though they had something to hide." But it was decided that clinical diagnoses were most effectively made on the basis of a total personality configuration, as observed through time, and in front of a uniform background. When the background was changed, the diagnostic confidence of the psychiatrist was diminished.

Clinical diagnoses of infantile conflicts are based to a large extent on what the patient says, as well as on how he looks and behaves, probably more on the basis of "noise" than on the basis of "information." That is, the clinician is keenly watching for, and listening for, inadvertent anxiety signals, as he absorbs the intended anamnesis given in his own way by the patient. If, during the first interview, the psychiatrist allows himself to subside into an attitude of free-floating attention, as he listens to and observes the patient, he may perceive the primal image—presented to him without any effort on his part. This image gives a great deal of information about what the patient is up to. No doubt the judgment of any psychiatrist concerning a new patient is a derivative of such a primal image, but in most cases it seems that the image itself is suppressed.

Under clinical conditions, the primal image consists of a picture of the patient in some infantile relationship to the psychiatrist, or, at any rate, to somebody. For example, in his mind's eye the psychiatrist sees him urinating on someone. He may have a certain revealing expression on his face as he does this, an expression which may have been observed during the interview. This image is often an accurate representation of an important archaic psychophysiological social striving of the patient. Later, in analysis, it may turn out to be an accurate picture of something that he actually remembers doing as a child, with the same expression on his face and the exact feeling signified by that expression. In one case the urination, in the psychiatrist's image, was accompanied by an expression of glee, which in subsequent interviews was observed to be characteristic of the patient. This image was probably derived from the psychiatrist's latent responses to the patient's stream of talk during the first interview. One day the patient remarked: "I turned the hose on my wife today as a joke. It reminds me of the time we put my little brother in a packing case and took turns urinating on him. I was about six at the time. My mother caught us and was very angry because I seemed to be enjoying it so much. I felt the same way with my wife. I realize now I feel that way when I corner somebody at a cocktail party and bore him to death with my talk. I like to pour it on."

A young woman suffering from anxiety hysteria had a smile which fascinated the psychiatrist. While he listened to her, he let the smile sink in. As she was telling a dream in which an older woman forced her to suck her breast, a rather unusual image appeared in the psychiatrist's mind. This image might be verbalized as follows: the patient, wearing her devilish smile, is tormenting a virile, sexually excited man by tickling him and refusing his importunities; then another man appears, again sexually excited, only this one is not robust like the other, but weak and miserable. The smile fades from the patient's face; she is overcome with sympathy, and is evidently going to satisfy this unfortunate creature. Later in the interview, the psychiatrist made some cautious inquiries. It seemed that she had an unusual sexual relationship with her husband; he and she would often spend a long time tickling each other until she was exhausted and he was violently excited, after which she would refuse intercourse. As a child, she and her sister used to get their father on the bed and tickle him (just as the woman in the dream got the patient on the bed). The psychiatrist remarked: "But if a man really needed your help, you would not withhold it." She then related a disagreeable experience. Just the other day she had picked up a pathetic looking hitchhiker and had treated him sympathetically. As a result, he had become so attached to her that he would come knocking on her door at all hours. He had finally become so persistent that she became frightened, and, to get rid of him, had had to threaten to call the police.

Sometimes when the image itself does not become conscious, the judgment appears in its primal form instead. In one case the doctor had the feeling: "This woman is 'unconsciously very conscious' of her anus." The patient later revealed a strong anal-erotic drive. Her most accessible traumatic experiences revolved around enemas which were forced on her by the family physician in the presence of her mother and grandmother.

A certain social worker gave the curious impression of walking around as if she were eternally waiting to get home and change her clothes because she had had an accidental bowel movement. The observer was very much interested in finding out why he had made such a disagreeable primal judgment concerning a person whom he held in some esteem. One day she spontaneously divulged that she had for years suffered from periodic colitis.

It has purposely been stressed that primal judgments in clinical practice are most effectively made during the initial interview. This is in accord with experience regarding intuition. It was found that, in general, a previous acquaintance with the agent was an obstacle in the way of diagnostic intuitive process. Intuitive accuracy tends to become clouded, in spite of the utmost efforts at objectivity, as the first impression of the agent is overlaid with clinical material and reactions provoked by defenses and security operations on both sides—the process of involvement between the patient and the psychiatrist. This can only be avoided if the therapeutic relationship is kept analytically pure and uncontaminated. Primal judgments properly belong to "the first 10 minutes," that decisive and important epoch in the development of any interpersonal relationships. ("The first 10 seconds," when the gross features of the physique, bearing, muscular coordination and mimicry are noted, is a slightly different topic.) Primal judgments come again to the fore when the "clouded" period of involvement has been successfully worked through, at which time Deutsch's statement (1944, p. 136) that intuition depends "on one's sympathy and love for and spiritual affinity with the other person" takes on its true connotations.

Primal judgments are particularly subject to distortion through countertransference. In such cases, the clinician finds himself with the same viewpoint as the patient; that is, his primal judgments are concerned, not with the patient's presenting problem, but with how suitable the patient is for the gratification of the therapist's own primal needs. Diagnostic primal images are the product of free-floating attention on the part of the therapist; if his attention is unconsciously directed to the possibilities for satisfaction of his own needs, his perceptions, and hence his diagnosis, and hence also, presumably, his therapeutic efforts will be distorted accordingly. Therapeutic effectiveness may be increased if undistorted primal images can gain access to the psychiatrist's awareness. Some therapists who are especially skillful with schizophrenics, such as Rosen (1947) and Fromm-Reichmann (1948), recognize this in different terms.

It is now easier to understand why the child, whose diagnostic ability often appears to have deadly accuracy, can sometimes be beguiled by a piece of candy. The moment his greed is appealed to, his judgment may be impaired. It is often the same with adults. From this point of view, a successful psychopath may be described as one skillful in inveigling his object's attention away from primal judgments while playing on primal needs. For example, the victim's primal judgment, "This man is going to bugger me," is clouded by a fog of communications deliberately designed by the psychopath to convey the impression: "Buggery is the last thing I would think of." In this way, the psychopath prepares the way for symbolic buggery of his victim, which is exactly what the victim unconsciously desires and anticipates. The efficacy of this system is demonstrated by the fact that a certain percentage of the victims of confidence men return and insist on trying again to "cheat the stockbroker," or whatever the game may be (Maurer, 1949).

Several discussants have mentioned their feeling that the writer has confused intuition and empathy. He does not believe that this is so. By intuition, he refers to a spontaneous diagnostic process whose end products spontaneously come into awareness if resistances are lifted. In the case of empathy, there are two classical definitions:

the aesthetic kind of projection of Worringer, based on Lipps, Jodl, and Wundt, and discussed at length by Jung (1946); and the Freudian concept of the deliberate, self-conscious "intellectual understanding of what is inherently foreign to our own Ego in other people" (Shatzky & Hinsie, 1940). Either way, empathy has a connotation of identification. Intuition, as the writer sees it, has essentially nothing to do with such adult forms of identification. It has to do with the automatic processing of sensory perceptions. It is primarily neither aesthetic nor intellectual, although it may be secondarily elaborated along these lines.

The writer came to consider these matters by a rather unusual path. He observed that in discussing the topic of intuition, some people exhibited what could only be interpreted as a dynamic resistance. Since resistance implies anxiety, the question arose as to what this particular group of people was afraid of. There must be something potentially dangerous hidden in this faculty. On the other hand, there is little doubt that many good clinicians profit from intuition, whether they are aware of it or not. Those who are aware of it sometimes attribute intuitive abilities to experience; they mean clinical experience. What is maintained here is that one type of intuitive process, here called primal judgments, is primarily based, not on clinical experience, but on forgotten infantile experience, so that the origin of primal judgments is not clearly manifest. The fact is that certain individuals feel insecure when they are not convinced that they have complete insight into their own cognitive processes.

Fenichel notes: "Schilder has shown that every single thought before formulation has gone through a prior wordless state . . . even in healthy, good thinkers who are wide awake, every single thought runs through initial phases that have more similarity with dream thinking than

with logic . . . thinking according to the primary process
. . . is carried out more through pictorial, concrete images, whereas the secondary process is based more on
words (1945, pp. 46 f.). He states that these images are
"less fitted for objective judgment," and are "full of
wishful or fearful misconceptions." (Ibid.)

Such anxieties may be strengthened by the observation
that one feature of certain schizophrenias is the tendency
to make primal judgments in their crudest form. Unless
this faculty is thoroughly under the control of the ego, it
may become pathogenic. Too much primal judgment
must be avoided. "Too much" is defined as more than the
percipient's ego is prepared to handle. Primal judgments
interfere with the information of spontaneous, healthy
relationships and find their legitimate usefulness mainly
in the clinical field.

From the same archaic substratum may arise highly
sublimated, socially valuable abilities, and corresponding
severely pathological disturbances. If dancing and
catatonia are related in this manner and if literature and
art are based on the same primal images which under
different conditions give rise to hebephrenic manifestations, then diagnosis and paranoia are similarly both
derived from primal judgments. Catatonia and hebe-
phrenia require only one individual; it takes two to make a
diagnosis or a paranoia, an agent and a percipient. Thus
diagnosis and paranoia both seem to be derivatives of
primal judgment. It can therefore be said that there is
nothing disreputable about intuition, since its most mys-
tifying manifestations are based on infantile experiences,
and for that reason are to be treated with respect, but also
with caution.

Ferenczi once remarked that education is not only the
acquisition of new faculties but is also the forgetting of
others, which, if not forgotten, would be supernormal

(ibid.). The patient himself is the best criterion for testing the validity of primal images and primal judgments.

Summary

1. Schizophrenia, borderline conditions, and neuroses often involve highly cathected, pathogenic images of a special type, which are archaic relics from infancy and childhood and have not undergone the normal processes of modification and resolution. Some (or all) normal people also have a store of such primal images based on infantile experiences, but in this case they have been decathected, mastered, and effectively assimilated.

2. These images, whether conscious or unconscious, are sometimes (or always) activated in interpersonal relationships and are related to the formation of basic judgments concerning people encountered. In normal adults, under ordinary conditions, such primal judgments do not come directly into awareness; conscious judgments of other people are derivatives of primal judgments, modified by cultural and other influences.

3. Some forms of intuition are derivatives of primal judgments based on primal images. Such intuitions are thus derived from infantile experiences. Other forms may be based on later clinical experience.

4. The possible diagnostic value to the clinician of his own primal judgments is discussed.

5 The Ego Image

The Problem

AN EIGHT-YEAR-OLD BOY, vacationing at a ranch
in his cowboy suit, helped the hired man unsaddle a
horse. When they were finished, the hired man said,
"Thanks, cowpoke!" To which his assistant answered: "I'm
not really a cowpoke, I'm just a little boy."

This story epitomizes something which has to be understood in regard to a patient (or anyone else) to maintain
rational insight into the interpersonal relationship when it
is desirable. The patient who told it remarked: "That's just
the way I feel. Sometimes I feel that I'm not really a
lawyer, I'm just a little boy." Everything that was said to
this patient was overheard by both people: the adult
lawyer and the inner little boy. To anticipate the effect of
an intervention, therefore, it is necessary to know not
only what kind of adult one is talking to, but also what
kind of little boy. This man came from Nevada, and he
had a special system for avoiding depression when he was
gambling. If he won, he would feel duly elated. If he lost,
say $50, he would tell himself: "I was prepared to lose
$100 tonight and I've only lost $50, so I'm really $50 ahead
and I needn't be upset." Often, especially if he was
winning, he would take a shower, after visiting one

casino, before he visited another, as if to wash away his guilt so he could feel "lucky" once more.

It is evident that there were two kinds of arithmetic employed here: When he was winning, that of a rational adult; when he was losing, that of a child with an archaic method of handling reality (denial). The taking of the shower represented a lack of confidence on the part of the "child." He did not trust the rational, well-thought-out, and rather effective gambling system of the "adult." The shower was part of a primitive, autistic contract the "child" made with the powers of gambling, in order to obtain license to win again.*

It was difficult to deal effectively with this patient without understanding these two different aspects of his personality. They were both conscious and both belonged to the ego system. One part of his personality faced reality as a whole, the other took it bit by bit and, by convenient manipulation, managed to find comfort in distressing situations, and anxiety in comforting ones. One part handled reality rationally, the other exploited it in an archaic way. There was no immediate question of the conscious versus the unconscious, or of ego versus id, in the sense of parapraxis or ego-dystonic behavior. Each approach made good sense in its own way: One was appropriate for the mature ego, the other was appropriate for a more primitive one. Conscious and unconscious, ego and id, were all involved somehow; but what was observed directly and what was most apparent to the patient and to the observer was the existence of two different conscious ego states: one that of an adult, the other that of a child.

---

*The analysis of this behavior led directly into the areas explored by Bergler (1943, 1949) in his study of the psychology of gamblers, and does not concern the present discussion.

Clinical Significance

Now—to leave the corral and the casino and go to the couch—the same division into at least two ego states can be observed more or less easily, in every patient. Ned, the lawyer, was a sexually confused man who used to make remarks in his social life like the following: "Us girls have got to be careful not to drink too much." After he had been in therapy for some time and was becoming acquainted with his two ego states, he reported that he had had the following unspoken thought at a party: "If I were a girl (but I'm not a girl) I wouldn't drink too much." He understood what this meant. In the old days, the "child" had prompted the "adult" to say: "Us girls . . ." Now the "adult" objected to the promptings of the "child" in two ways: "I'm not a girl," and, "I don't intend to make remarks about it aloud in any case."

In this example, the patient conveniently offered material which indicated what was going on and what kind of "child" had to be dealt with. In other cases, the situation is more obscure, and it requires a considerable degree of clinical intuition to make the psychological dissection required to separate the "child" from the "adult."

In [the preceding papers] . . . the writer has discussed the nature of intuitive processes, their functions in diagnosis and in the understanding of latent communications, and their phenomenological reality as primal images. The present communication is intended to bring these processes into focus, as constituting a specific feature in clinical psychotherapy. A similar process of bringing into focus was undertaken in considering "primal images," the therapist's perception of the mode and zone of the patient's instinctual strivings as aroused in the therapeutic situation and directed toward the therapist. The present discussion will be of "ego images," which are specific perceptions of the patient's active archaic ego state in relation to the people around him. An illustration may help to clarify this.

Certain patients appear in practice who may be characterized at the outset as "severe latent homosexuals," or "latent paranoid schizophrenics." The primal image activated by such a patient may give rise to the primal judgment: "This man is concerned about buggery." That means that his instinctual position in relation to the therapist is an anal receptive one; he symbolically turns or avoids turning his buttocks. This is valuable information and may have considerable predictive usefulness as a guide over a long-term course of therapy. But its value is limited in the initial situation and in various complex digressions which may arise. The "ego image" complements the ultimate orientation given by the primal image. It offers a much more useful guide in the preliminary phases of treatment and in diluted forms of treatment, particularly in helping avoid unnecessary hostile responses whose significance might be clouded by labeling them "unexpected transference reactions." The same man who evokes the primal judgment: "He is concerned about buggery," may also elicit the following intuitive impression: "This man feels as though he were a very young child, standing naked and sexually excited before a group of his elders, blushing furiously and writhing with almost unbearable embarrassment." This is an image of the patient's ego state, and hence may be called an "ego image," just as the image activated by his instinctual strivings may be called a "primal image."

The primal image, then, refers to an instinctual orientation; the ego image refers to an ego state. It is difficult to apply usefully the first piece of information, "This man is concerned about buggery." At the beginning, all one can do is refrain from threatening him, either actually or symbolically; at the end, it becomes a highly technical and complex matter to use the information advantageously and therapeutically. The second message is more useful: "He is writhing inwardly with almost unbearable embarrassment." From the moment this message is perceived, it can be profitably applied in the immediate situation.

Doubts as to proper technique can be resolved by asking oneself: "What would I say or do if a three-year-old child who was writhing with embarrassment behaved the way this patient is doing?" This is a much easier question to answer than: "What do you do if a passive anal homosexual behaves in this way?" Furthermore, it seems simpler to detect and control countertransference tendencies toward an embarrassed three-year-old child than toward a passive homosexual adult, if only because the former is for most people a more congenial figure. Both the primal image and the ego image represent aspects of the "child," and together they form a useful guide at all stages of therapy.

Ordinarily, of course, one does not discuss such intuitions with patients until the footing is secure, if at all; but the therapist keeps them continuously in mind, and they control his behavior. Diana, a young housewife-student who was perceived in just the squirming way described, had had two psychotic breaks requiring hospitalization during a five-year period (1946-1951): one before she came to the therapist and the second a year after she had interrupted therapy. During her first therapeutic period, she was treated according to the principle: "This is a woman with strong homosexual conflicts and strong anal receptive strivings." For example, her heterosexual genital attitudes were encouraged; but this was not enough.

In the five years after the therapist focused on perception of her ego state (1951-1956), she required no further hospitalization. Furthermore, when she had broken down in 1949 after leaving therapy, the therapist had been involved in her delusions as a hostile conspirator. During the second phase, when she became disturbed on two occasions after discontinuing her treatment temporarily there were two differences from the 1949 break: First, the therapist was cast in the role of a beneficent conspirator so that she felt safe, because he was arranging for her to be safe at all times; and, second, her mature ego (the "adult") had been strengthened sufficiently so that she did not break down, and so that she recognized her troublesome feelings as delusions, the revival of an archaic ego state (cf. Federn, 1952). As a result, she was able to carry on her work and her studies efficiently enough to keep her household going and to pass her examinations with a good grade, even during periods when she was engaged in an acute struggle with her paranoia. And there was something much more specific at work here than a mere orthodox shift from "id therapy" to "ego therapy."

In Diana's case, it became possible to investigate the accuracy of the intuitive ego image. After being treated once weekly for two years according to the principle, "Remember she is a child, writhing with embarrassment," rather than, "Remember the homosexual and anal conflicts," she was introduced to a therapy group. After a year in the group, it became possible to mention to her how the therapist perceived her ego state. A couple of weeks later she reported that she had been much impressed by this conception of herself and had given it a good deal of thought. The therapist had gained his insight one day by carefully observing her manner in the office, and thus far had no historical grounds for his intuition. She now offered the following material:

"I don't remember this myself but my mother told me about it. I was playing in our back yard. For some reason my diaper was off and I was naked. A group of men were watching me over the fence and laughing. My mother came out to see what it was all about. She got very embarrassed when she saw what was happening and hustled me into the house. I can imagine how embarrassed she was, because she still undresses behind a screen."

This story, which is most likely a secondhand account of a repressed screen memory, was the first evidence that the ego image had a historical basis. Yet the patient's response to the therapist's revised attitude had already indicated that his intuition was correct.* The therapist, on his part, had had enough confidence in his intuition throughout to adhere to it, even when this made difficulties with the other members of the therapy group because of alleged "favoritism." But by treating each member of the group according to the indications offered by his respective ego image, these difficulties were overcome. The real problem arose with members of whom he was unable to obtain clear ego images.

A Clinical Example

One may now observe in some detail how the attainment of a clear ego image improved a rather chaotic and unfavorable therapeutic situation. The case concerns a 40-year-old woman in whose case the primal image was clear enough from the beginning: She was wallowing in feces and was involved in a powerful conflict about how far she could go in defecating, with generosity as well as with malice, all over the therapist. The difficulty was, however, that at the time the treatment began, the therapist

---

*At the time of going to press, the patient has been married for six months and is functioning happily as a housewife.

did not know about ego images; or in more ordinary terms, did not perceive the patient's ego state concretely enough, although it was sufficiently clear in an academic, inferential way.

This patient, Emily, was referred for treatment of severe, frequent, and long-lasting hemicrania, with scotomata and sometimes vomiting. She had spent a great deal of time during the preceding 15 years looking for and trying various remedies without relief, including a year of psychotherapy three times a week. For cogent reasons, she could only be seen regularly twice a week by the writer—occasionally three times weekly—hardly an encouraging program for such a refractory case. Nevertheless, after three years her condition was considerably ameliorated—the headaches rarely occurred—and she reported that she got along better in several types of situations.

For the first two years, however, the improvement had been superficial, unstable, and sporadic, because of lack of insight on both sides. It was only after the therapist obtained a clear-cut ego image that the course of therapy could be controlled with some understanding and precision.

This patient showed many depressive symptoms: weeping spells, suicidal fantasies, sensitiveness with resentment, and depression itself. She was tyrannically self-depreciating, guilt ridden, passively aggressive, and masochistic. Her defenses were weak, spotty, and poorly organized: There was obsessive cleanliness combined with untidiness; there was a strong but inefficient effort to appear cultured and well-bred; and she was stubborn, yet panicky. Demands for sympathy from her husband were easily smashed. There was sporadic alcoholism, and a continual quest for new medications, which she did not take regularly. She made aggressive threats, coupled with abject compliance; and she exhibited righteousness, combined with crafty deceptiveness. If these trends had been firmly established, they could have been dealt with, but they lacked stability and integration. The picture was not so "hard" as it sounds. The whole defensive system was "soft" to the point of mushiness, giving the clinical impression that it could not be dealt with, but only wallowed in.

At the slightest sign of danger, Emily relinquished one defense and sank into another. Interpretation failed, because she could see it coming. She experienced it as "name calling," and would obviate it by calling herself names first. If interpretations were withheld, she felt lonely, neglected, and suicidal. "Support"—if she did not succeed in finding criticism in it—made her feel guilty and more depressed.

During this phase, the patient was much more satisfied with her progress than the therapist was. She did not want to transfer to another psychotherapist or another form of treatment.

The behavior of the therapist during this period was guided to some extent by an academic, inferential and rather stereotyped "ego model," which remained unformulated and preconscious. This model characterized the patient in a banal, barren, and obvious way in such terms as vulnerable, apprehensive, conventional—seeking justification for resentment, self-pity, and self-castigation. This perceptual skeleton, fleshless though it was, had undoubtedly exerted a helpful controlling influence on whatever progress had been made. But evidently its value as the basis for a live therapy was low, even if a new bone could be added to the frame from time to time.

Then one day she remarked: "I was a bloody mess when I was born and a disappointment to my parents because I was a girl." This report, typical for this kind of patient, was of little practical value. But later in the hour she added: "My mother told me that I disgusted her when I was wet, and she hated to pick me up. But she said my Uncle Charlie would cuddle me even when I was dripping. He didn't mind picking me up at all. She used to say to him: 'How can you hold her when she's in that disgusting condition?' "

This was probably a secondhand account of a repressed screen memory, as in the case, noted before, of Diana's nakedness. It immediately brought the whole situation into better focus. It told the therapist how Emily felt, and it told him how he must behave. Things began to go more smoothly. Everything was now more understandable, controllable, and predictable; that is, the treatment proceeded with only the usual errors and oversights on the part of the therapist. His groping and his feeling of inadequacy gave way to a well-oriented therapeutic plan.

The descriptive ego model was now replaced by a substantial ego image. Emily was no longer a set of verbal concepts but a clearly pictured personality. She was an infant with a dripping diaper, shrinking from her mother's disgust and tyrannical castigation, and looking for an uncle to hold her as she was. The therapist had only to be that uncle, and the situation would improve. He was, and it did. Countertransference reactions became simpler to detect and avert. Transference reactions became easier to understand, to predict, to control, and to work with.

The therapist could now ask himself: "How does she expect this uncle to behave?" in order to know what to do and what not to do; and, "What does she want from this uncle?" in order to understand what the patient was doing in the treatment. There were, of course, many aspects to be tested. The ego image had to be refined in the crucible of experience. After a few months, the situation could be understood as follows: "The uncle who is holding this little wet infant must avoid a great many things, such as letting on that he knows she is wet. He must make it clear that he will hold her even when her mother will not—and that he will do so without betraying her, scolding her, seducing her. If he fulfills these conditions, she will gossip to him about all sorts of things and even tell him secrets more and more terrible that she could never tell anyone else."

This ego image was not mentioned to the patient, for that might have damaged its usefulness. Her account of the Uncle Charlie incident was allowed to pass without comment, and the therapist did not refer to it again. There was plenty of other material available for the exploration of her urinary problems. In the ensuing months, her headaches lessened in frequency, intensity, and duration, she began to hold her own with other people, and was able to talk more and more freely about her early anal conflicts and even about her current anal masturbation; these were all noteworthy accomplishments for her. All this, of course, was related to "transference improvement."

It will be noted that this approach referred entirely to her ego state and took no account of her id strivings in relation to this uncle. It was clear, however, that sooner or later her desire to urinate and defecate on the uncle would have to be broached; that is, the ego image as a guide to therapeutic technique would have to give way before the primal image. The ego image served its function in the transitional stage between establishing a clear relationship and beginning progressive, well-oriented therapy, and one could always fall back on it in times of stress.

To clarify the situation in review: The ego image served as a technical guide in approaching the suggestive picture presented by the primal image. Three years of experience indicated that the only person to whom she could possibly reveal her wallowing in feces, her coprophilia, and her soiling impulses, was someone who treated her like an uncle; and then only when she was securely assured of his benevolent fidelity. In the hands of two different therapists, no other technique had succeeded with this patient. Nearly everybody agrees that special techniques are necessary in order to do analytic work with patients who are basically close to psychosis. On the other hand, this present technique was not a corrective emotional experience, in the sense of Alexander. It was a repetition of a good infantile experience.

A new phase began when the patient moved decisively from the urinary to the anal sphere. The old ego image then lost its value, and the therapist once more became uncertain of his position. He had to fall back again for guidance on an academic, descriptive ego model. An incident when the patient was put out on the doorstep for soiling her bed was not of much value since it merely indicated what was easy to see anyway, that she was afraid of being thrown out if she had "dirty" thoughts. This episode did not distinguish her as an idiosyncratic individual in relationship with other idiosyncratic individuals, as the Uncle Charlie situation did. It gave no clear, substantial picture of her ego state and, therefore, could not serve as the basis for an ego image. Because no ego image came to light to serve as a guide during this phase, the third stage of her treatment proceeded in a less coherent way.

Incidentally, the accuracy of the primal image, in which she was defecating all over the therapist, was confirmed during the later phase. On two occasions when she had diarrhea, she soiled her husband slightly during intercourse just when she reached orgasm. She described her feelings as a mixture of great pleasure and great disgust. (The final therapeutic outcome of this case is not determined yet.)

Ego Model, Ego Symbol, and Image

From the foregoing, it can be seen that the ego image comes to life with varying degrees of difficulty with different patients. Sometimes it never comes to life at all. Experience up to this point indicates that in general it offers itself most easily in cases of latent schizophrenia and least readily in cases of complicated character neuroses. The patient himself is probably rarely, if ever, aware of it, or at least of its significance, since in verified cases it seems to be based on secondhand accounts of repressed screen memories; and such things seem of little importance to the patient, because the affect is not accessible to him. But increasing experience gives the therapist more and more hints as to where to look in various types of cases. Such experience is worth cultivating, since, as Emily's case demonstrates, the attainment of a clear ego image in the therapist's mind may be crucial for the progress of the therapy, especially in regard to time.

How is the ego image picked out? This is a topic which is difficult to clarify. In the case of latent paranoid schizophrenics, as well as in other diagnostic categories if the same kind of archaic embarrassment is present, the patient's squiriming may be observed in a larval form, and a question about erythrophobia may confirm the perception of the "child's" ego state. In a case such as Emily's, where the therapist has no precedent, it is simply the fact that all sorts of vague impressions and academic conceptions regarding the patient seem to crystallize, come to life, and become highly intelligible when the right note is struck. Evidently the therapist's intuitive readiness has a great deal to do with picking out of the enormous mass of firsthand and secondhand memories precisely the one which can serve as a beacon to guide him at every step in the right direction. Beyond this, little can be said now; the explanation must await further studies of the intuitive process itself.

In practice, if he is fortunate, the therapist may find himself at a certain moment holding in his mind an image by means of which he can evaluate his own reactions, sort out therapeutic and contratherapeutic attitudes, predict with considerable success how the patient will react to what he says, and understand why she is reacting in a certain way to what he has said. In Emily's case, for example, the therapist found it wise to reject all "unavuncular" reactions on his part and act only upon "avuncular" ones; while at the same time he tried to avoid obviously avuncular statements, because these might sound seductive or too revealing and so spoil the therapeutic situation. At a later phase, the ego image loses its usefulness, and the therapist is once more on his own, with only academic knowledge, clinical experience, and the primal image to guide him; but now he is on a more secure footing than at the start, and the patient may tolerate a good deal of misjudgment on his part—a relaxing and encouraging situation for an average therapist.

If a convincing ego image is not forthcoming in a given case, the therapist need not feel lost, since there are two worthwhile substitutes. The first is the "ego model" already referred to. This is a descriptive perception of the patient, an additive rather than a holistic one, an atomistic series of propositions rather than a gestalt. The ego model came to perhaps its highest flower in the work of Eugen Kahn (1931), with his "heuristic system of psychopathies according to the clinico-descriptive method," resulting in an exquisitely sensitive and detailed set of such models. Kahn later attributed to each of these types its own "way of experiencing," thus adding to the usefulness of his descriptions.

The second type of substitute may be called an "ego symbol." This is intermediate between an ego model and an ego image. Its nature may be illustrated by two examples.

1. A young woman gave at the first interview with the therapist a strong impression of being extremely frightened underneath, although on the surface she presented herself rather well as a sophisticated, competent, and well-integrated person. Unhappily, the history tended to confirm the therapist's impression of intense underlying anxiety. But for two months in treatment she maintained her good front. Then one day she came in with a clipping from a magazine, an advertisement for frozen chicken. The drawing depicted a plucked chicken lying on a couch, apparently comfortable and relaxed, waiting cheerfully to be cooked and eaten. This picture reproduced the patient's attitude on the couch so accurately and made her underlying feelings, even her resigned cheerfulness, so clear that both patient and therapist burst out laughing. From that time on, the therapist treated her with the kind of consideration she would be entitled to if she were really in the unfortunate chicken's situation, and the results were gratifying. (This may be characterized as a "counter-cannibalistic" attitude on the part of the therapist, in the face of what now appeared to be provocative behavior from the patient.) This picture was not so good as a guide as a more personal ego image but it served its purpose well as a symbol of how the patient felt and as a guide in therapeutic technique.

2. An intelligent, imaginative, and socially productive schizoid man gave a large number of responses on his

initial Rorschach examination. Two of these in particular attracted the therapist's attention: "a worm" and "a dried-up insect." The therapist adopted these tentatively as ego symbols and from the beginning treated the patient with the kind of consideration due to one who felt no more worthy than a worm and no more alive than a dried-up insect. Of course the therapist gave the patient no hint of his thoughts on the matter. Shortly afterward the patient spontaneously began to interlard his productions with occasional associations about worms and dried-up insects, usually in connection with incidents where he was treated in a humiliating or neglectful way. At first, everything the therapist said and did was guided by the principle: "Would this be therapeutic if it were applied to a worm or a dried-up insect?" At times, it was possible to judge even which ego symbol applied at a given moment; during one hour, it would be necessary to do "worm therapy," and a few hours later, "dried-up insect therapy." The reader may well ask, "What is worm therapy?" and, "What is dried-up insect therapy?" These are questions to which verbal answers cannot be formulated. Nevertheless, one intuitively knows how to avoid hurting humiliated worms and neglected insects and how to help them on their evolutionary way toward humanity. It is a little different, for example, from helping a plucked chicken on her way to becoming an effective woman.

In the writer's experience, one of the chief clinical values of a Rorschach report is that it may yield important symbolic information regarding the patient's ego state; such information may serve as a significant guide in therapeutic technique and may be particularly welcome if a good ego image is not forthcoming.

Interestingly enough, in the two cases cited, the ego symbols appeared spontaneously in the patients' associations during treatment but did not occur in their dreams.

Neither did the "squirming child" of Diana or the "dripping infant" of Emily appear in those patients' dreams.

On the theoretical side, the ego model is descriptive. The ego symbol is related to Silberer's functional phenomenon (1951) and can be discussed in terms of Jones's ideas about symbols (1923). The ego image finds its theoretical basis in Federn's ideas, summarized as follows by Weiss: "That ego configurations of former age levels are maintained in potential existence within one's personality is experimentally proven, since they can be re-cathected directly under special conditions; for instance, in hypnosis, in dreams, and in psychosis. In fact, Federn recognized that every morning, upon awakening, the ego undergoes a rapid repetition of its development from birth. He introduced a new term to indicate this process, *orthriogenesis*" (1950, p. 80). What is maintained by Federn is that many neurotics and latent psychotics are fixated, not only libidinally but also in their ego states. (From the descriptive point of view, this is also Kahn's "way of experiencing.") The ego image thus functions as an intuitively selected paradigm of the patient's ego fixation, which, according to Federn's terminology, would constitute "incomplete orthriogenesis." The ego symbol and the ego model are less plastic representations of the same thing. Therapy in this light then involves completing the orthriogenesis; and, as this ego therapy proceeds, the libidinal fixations can also be dealt with according to the indications.

One more item is worth considering: the application of the ego image and the primal image to everyday life. One can infer that the kinematic basis of interpersonal relationships is mutual intuitive understanding through partial ego images and primal images even though these may never become conscious. That is, any two people in any kind of ongoing relationship behave *as though* they were acting in accordance with ego images and primal images (cf. chap. 2); and the more congenial or complementary these images, the more chance that the relationship will survive certain kinds of reality difficulties—or so it seems. In this connection, the ego image is what seems to be related to and worked with in everyday life; while the primal image shows what is strongly or ambivalently defended against—that is, what kind of seduction is to be feared or ambivalently permitted. Emily's friends accept her and listen to her, and she loves them for it, just as she did her uncle; but they sidestep her symbolic attempts to defecate upon them. Very likely there is some competition in her circle in the latter sphere. Sensible people protect latent paranoid schizophrenics from embarrassment in accordance with the ego image, but they avoid unwholesome entanglements with them, warned by the primal image, even if, as is usually the case, both images remain unconscious. If the "sensible people" fail in either respect, the relationship will either not proceed well or will become extraordinarily complicated and no longer a matter of everyday life. Similar considerations apply to the relationships between more stable people.

Therapeutic Application

To return to the original example of Ned, the gambling lawyer, where there seemed to be a "child" and an "adult," how does one treat such a person? If one talks sensibly, the "adult" will understand, but the "child" will subject what is said to his own peculiar rules of logic. If one talks babytalk, both the "child" and the "adult" will justifiably become indignant. Both croupiers and psychiatrists have to know this. Such a person must be spoken to like an adult but treated like a child. To succeed in this, it is necessary to know what kind of child one is dealing with. This does not mean giving in to the child, but does mean "treating" the child in the clinical sense.

In fact, careful observation indicates that this therapeutic principle applies to all patients. The colleague who first helped to clarify this was a pediatrician. It soon appeared that the psychiatrist's professional position was similar to his, something like that, in fact, of a pediatrician who has to treat a serious family problem in a one-room cabin in the middle of winter. Since neither the mother nor the child can be sent out of the room, everything that is said to the mother will be overheard and scanned by the anxiously alert child who is confusedly fighting with all his strength for emotional survival; and everything that is said to the child will fall on the defensive ears of the mother. Under these conditions, therapeutic control can only be maintained by an adequate knowledge of the psychology of both the individual adult and the individual child. It is not enough to say or do what is appropriate only for the mother; if the child is alarmed by it, the situation is not improved or will deteriorate; nor is it enough to say only what is appropriate for the child, for if the mother is not reassured by it, she may become increasingly defensive.

In the psychiatric situation, the adult and the child are contained in the same individual. It is true that the "child" can be cowed sometimes by an authoritative or threatening attitude (there are indications that shock treatment may fall into this class), or that the "adult" can be "sent out of the room" by the use of certain pharmacological and other procedures (narcoanalysis and hypnosis), but sooner or later the decommissioned part of the personality returns, and then the fat is in the fire. In rational psychotherapy, it is necessary to deal with both simultaneously. The "adult" responds to the rationality (by definition, so to speak) and does not constitute a

117

problem. The "child" responds to the therapy, and it is here that the therapist's experience, knowledge, attitude, and intuition have their value. The most effective way to control the situation is by means of a valid ego image. It has already been indicated that neurotics are most difficult to work with in this respect, since the ego image does not seem to emerge so readily as in other patients, and the therapist may have to be content with an ego model or an ego symbol. It is particularly in the most difficult classes of patients, such as psychopaths, "acting-outers," schizoids, latent schizophrenics, and the mentally retarded, that an ego image is most likely to be accessible. In other words, the ego image is easiest to attain just in those cases where it is most needed and where it will do the most good. In any case, every psychiatrist has to function as a child psychiatrist, even if his practice is confined to adults.

The therapist who works with ego images for a year or two will eventually run into a complication. He will find that there are not two, but several, ego states that have to be taken into account for more precise work. While the child-adult framework gives excellent results in many types of cases, it is possible to go farther. But this subject belongs in the field of psychotherapy and is no longer something which pertains primarily to the problem of intuition, [as Chapter 6 will indicate].

In the present series of studies concerned with intuition, covering a period of 10 years, a bridge has been built from "guessing games" about soldiers' occupations over to the intuitive understanding of patients and the use of intuition as a psychotherapeutic tool in a specific framework. The clinical examples given show that perhaps none of the conclusions is new; but something may have been learned through reaching them by a rather unusual approach.

Summary

1. The intuitive understanding of patients is phenomenologically manifested in two kinds of images: primal images, which refer to predominant modes and zones of instinctual striving; and ego images, which refer to fixations in the patient's ego state.

2. Ego images, in the writer's experience, are most readily forthcoming in cases of latent psychosis.

3. Ego images, ego symbols, and ego models are distinguished as guiding influences in therapy; each of them is useful to a certain degree in understanding a patient's regressive ego state and the therapist's reaction to it. Ego images represent Federn's approach, ego symbols Silberer's, and ego models Kahn's.

4. Ego images and primal images also have their influence on the interpersonal relationships of everyday life.

5. Ego images help the therapist to clearly distinguish archaic ego functioning from mature ego functioning. For convenience, these aspects of functioning are called the "child" and the "adult" in the patient.

6. The psychiatrist's position is similar to that of a pediatrician who cannot send either the mother or the child out of the room. Thus every psychotherapist must function simultaneously as a child therapist and an adult therapist, even if his practice is confined to adults.

6 Ego States in Psychotherapy

I N VIEW OF the number of patients in treatment each year, there is no need to stress the importance of research (as contrasted with surveys) in psychotherapy. The approach described below seems to find its most useful application in just those cases where other methods of psychotherapy are generally considered to be the most difficult or least effective: for example, in ambulatory schizophrenia, depressions, manic-depressive psychoses in remission, alcoholism, borderline intelligence, psychopathic personalities, and acting out personalities in general. It has been most gratifying to observe again and again the rapidity and effectiveness with which psychopathology and acting out can be circumscribed by the use of this system. Equally interesting is the relative ease with which it can be taught. In group therapy, after a variety of therapeutic experiments over a period of 13 years, it has also proved to be the most productive approach.

A Clinical Illustration

. . . The patient who told [the cowpoke] story remarked: "That's just the way I feel. I'm not really a lawyer, I'm just a little boy." Away from the psychiatrist's office, this 35-year-old man was an effective and successful courtroom lawyer of high repute, who raised his family decently, did a lot of useful community work, and was popular socially. But in treatment, he often did have the attitude of a little boy. Sometimes during his hour he would ask "Are you talking to the lawyer or to the little boy?" As we both became interested in this question, it became possible to distinguish more and more clearly the two attitudes, so that he was often able to say whether it was "the lawyer" or "the little boy" who was talking at any given moment. But sometimes he seemed to misperceive, so that it had to be pointed out to him that what he diagnosed as the lawyer's attitude really appeared to be more like that of a little boy.

Quite soon, we were speaking familiarly of these two attitudes as "the adult" and "the child." The therapeutic task then became to separate out more clearly the adult from the child. As this work proceeded, there were noteworthy changes in his mode of living, without any direct suggestion. His psychopathology receded almost completely from his daily life and was confined to weekend sprees. The whiskey bottle, the lewd pictures, the guns and the morphine (which he was keeping for a projected "psychological experiment") were moved out of his home and office and into the weekend hideout to which he retired every month or so for "fishing." The danger of complete ruin was now greatly diminished. His home life changed to such an extent that his wife, his children, and his friends all commented upon it. Later, as treatment progressed over a period of four years, the morphine was thrown away, the whiskey bottle was put aside, and his private perversion came under much better control.

All this might be labeled mere "symptomatic relief,"

but there are certain details of interest. The technical mechanism of this improvement was based on the patient's increasing ability to distinguish the "child" from the "adult." What he actually did, in this terminology, was to keep the "adult" in control all week, at the expense of the "child." The "child" was then allowed to express his mounting tension over the weekend, when it was relatively harmless. The patient during this phase had learned to distinguish two different ego states.

An "ego state" may be described phenomenologically as a coherent system of feelings, and operationally as a set of coherent behavior patterns; or pragmatically, as a system of feelings which motivates a related set of behavior patterns. This patient had one ego state wherein he felt like a lawyer and acted like a lawyer, and another wherein he felt like a masochistic child *of a certain age* and acted like such a child. At the beginning, these two ego states were overlapped and interwoven, as in *Figure 1a*. At the end, they had been dissected apart, as in *Figure 1b*. The therapeutic operation consisted of defining and strengthening the boundary between them.

This operation resulted in a special kind of insight. At first, the patient thought that the boundary of the "adult" was represented by the heavy line in *Figure 2a*. He did not realize that because of overlapping, this boundary included part of the "child." This meant that certain irrational elements in his behavior were perceived by him as rational, and were ego-syntonic: in the present language, "adult ego" syntonic. For example, the "child" wanted his secretary to find the morphine and the lewd pictures in his unlocked desk, in order that she might take the (magic) hint and share his perversions. The "adult" perceived this indiscretion as rational: if he locked his desk, she might get suspicious and break it open, and so forth. The initial insight may be represented by *Figure*

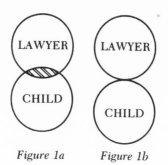

Figure 1a   Figure 1b

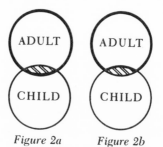

Figure 2a   Figure 2b

2*b*, where the area of overlapping between the "adult" and the "child" is now excluded from the boundary of the adult ego state; so that, for example, his rationalization for the unlocked desk was no longer acceptable to the "lawyer."

In other words, he learned to accept as adult only what was completely rational, in the sense of psychologically and materially realistic, in his judgment of his environment and the probable effect of his behavior upon it. The irrational attitudes, meanwhile, remained ego-syntonic also, but specifically "child ego" syntonic. Thus little was changed at this stage except the boundary between the two ego states. He could distinguish clearly what was "adult" and what was "not adult." This was the first step in changing his behavior. He could now relegate the "child's" self-expression to a more appropriate time and place. Until he was aware of this distinction in its details he could not do this, since the "child's" influence could always creep into his behavior without his realizing what had happened, because part of the "child" (the contaminated area in *Figure 2a*) was accepted as being within the "adult" ego boundary.

In nosologic terms, an unstable schizoid personality *(Figure 2a)* had been transformed into a stable "weekend schizophrenic" *(Figure 2b)*. There were two advantages to this: First, it probably saved him from the impending social calamity which had brought him to treatment; secondly, the "purified adult ego" was a much improved instrument for dealing therapeutically with the "unhealthy child," which was the core of his illness, and which had now been corralled, so to speak, in the weekend hideout.

The process of clearly differentiating ego states, which may be conveniently called "structural analysis," should be clearly distinguished at this point from two of its therapeutic relatives. It is different from an "ego" vs. "id" approach because, as will be explained shortly, the "child" is not synonymous with the id, but is a complete ego state in itself, with its own psychic structure. And on the other hand, this method does not merely attempt to teach the patient to see his environment more realistically; it deals with his internal perceptions as well as his external perceptions, in an attempt to free his own good judgment from contamination by archaic attitudes; his purified adult ego can then proceed on its own to handle things correctly.

What Federn (1952) calls "a mental duologue between two parts of the ego, the adult and the infantile," becomes clearer when the boundaries between two ego states become well defined and both are in an active state. The sexually confused lawyer used to make remarks in his social life like the following: "Us girls have got to be careful not to drink too much." After the boundary between his "adult" and his "child" became well defined, he reported that he had had the following thoughts at a party: "If I were a girl (but I'm not a girl) I wouldn't drink too much (but I don't intend to make remarks about it aloud in any case)." The phrases in parentheses are the "adult's" gloss on the "child's" wisdom, and saved him from regret, from embarrassment, and from adding another item to the dangerously mounting gossip about him in the community. In the old days, the contaminated "adult" (shaded figure of *Figure 1a*) would say: "Us girls . . ." etc. Now the masculine, sensible, purified "adult" distinguished himself from the bisexual impulsive "child." When the "child" thought: "Us girls . . ." etc., the adult was no longer taken in, and made the two realistic objections given in the parentheses.

Meanwhile a new complication arose. After about a year it became evident that certain of his attitudes did not belong to either the "child" or the "adult," as we increased our understanding of those components. These anomalous attitudes were collected and crystallized into a third ego state which came to be called the "parent," since they were evidently a reflection of parental prejudices. His parents were pious people, and throughout his childhood had exhorted him to "do good and never have a mean thought." At such times as the patient adopted the outlook of one of his parents, he exhibited the complete ego state of that parent, or at least his version of it. He not only rebuked himself (i.e., his "child") for having "mean thoughts," but he talked about handling money the way his father had, rather than the way he himself, as an adult lawyer, was accustomed to do.

In fact, each component had its own way of handling money. The "child" was penurious to the penny and had miserly ways of ensuring penny-wise prosperity; the "adult" handled thousands of dollars with a banker's shrewdness, foresight, and success, and was willing to spend money to make money; the "parent" had fantasies of giving it all away for the good of the community, and the patient actually was philanthropically generous in imitation of his parents, which caused the "child" to squirm resentfully and the "adult" to wonder. Thus in matters of money, for example, the "dialogue" became a "trialogue." The patient would slip from one to another of these attitudes, and we soon learned to recognize which was which.

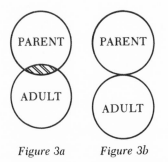

Figure 3a   *Figure 3b*

The next phase of the patient's therapy was to decontaminate the "adult" from the "parental" influence. He had to learn, for example, that his policy of using enemas in bowel training was familial, and not necessarily rational as he had previously maintained. The boundary between the "parent" and the "adult" had to be redefined in exactly the same way as the boundary between the "adult"

127

and the "child," as illustrated in *Figures 3a* and *3b*. The final result, as far as ego states are concerned, is illustrated in *Figure 4b*, where the "parent," the "adult," and the "child" all have well-defined boundaries, as contrasted with the initial state, represented in *Figure 4a*, where the "adult" is contaminated from both sides, so that in certain areas "child" and "parent" attitudes are "adult ego" syntonic. The net effect of all this was that now the doubly "purified adult ego state" could stand aside, as it were, and watch the continuing battle between the "child" and the "parent" with greatly increased objectivity and clarity: an advantageous therapeutic position.

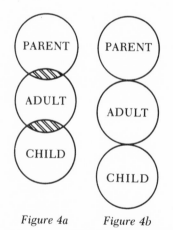

Figure 4a   Figure 4b

The further course of therapy in such cases is a matter of judgment. The therapist has a valuable ally in the "purified adult ego." The actual psychopathology for the most part resides in the "child." In this case the "child" was hostile, easily panicked, sexually confused, and afraid that something would be taken away from him; the "adult" was intelligent and realistic; and the "parent" was weak and sentimental. The problem was to allay the "child's" anxiety and "unconfuse" him so that he would contribute charm, humor, freshness, and masculinity to the total personality. He must be brought to terms with the "adult" and the "parent" without arousing his hostility, and receive in return more healthy freedom and protection.

The therapist proceeded to do this as tactfully as he could. During this phase, if the "child" felt threatened or offended, he let the doctor know it through an emotional outburst; if the "adult" was not satisfied, he offered a rational objection or showed a manly indignation at the therapist's ineptness or forgetfulness; if the "parent's" standards were slighted, he (or she) became primly righteous. But the therapist kept in mind always that all three parties would be listening alertly to everything he said and that none of them could be sent out of the room for even a moment.

The outcome was as successful as anyone could hope for in a case of this kind, as the patient himself pointed out. He was not only saved from what was probably an impending social and psychological calamity, and perhaps suicide, but his life was also improved in many spheres. He made his own diagnosis of the "child's" psychotic condition when he became better acquainted with this aspect of his personality. But this did not lead to despair, since at the same time he was able to feel the increasing clarity and confidence of his "adult."

Subjectively, the result was in increased feeling of inner harmony. Behaviorally, he learned to hold his own when "parent," "adult," and "child" were all agreed, first by learning where they could agree, and then by selecting his activities in such a way that concerted effort on the part of all three was appropriately directed so as to give universal satisfaction. Instead of thinly spread community work, some of which was compatible to one component while at the same time arousing petulance, cynicism, or ethical doubts in another, he began to concentrate on activities which gratified all three simultaneously: the "child's" exhibitionism, the "adult's" intellectual curiosity and sense of accomplishment, and the "parent's" philanthropy.

The reason this man improved visibly and subjectively was because of his real insight. This was not merely an intellectual acceptance of a set of concepts; he could actually perceive, as psychological realities, the three ego states which were in conflict inside of him, as in matters of money for example. He recognized with conviction in the "child" actual attitudes from his earliest childhood, and in the "parent" actual attitudes of his mother and father, and could pick out the real autonomies which went to make up the "adult."

Some Necessary Theoretical Considerations

A review of the literature reveals that some of the concepts which emerged through the use of this method were anticipated by Federn (1952) in his ego psychology. What is new, therefore, as is so often the case, is not necessarily the concepts, but the emphasis and development. A detailed consideration of the theoretical background belongs to a separate communication, but a certain minimum is necessary for practical understanding before moving on to further clinical examples in an attempt to make the matter clearer. (In the following discussion it is more convenient to capitalize *Parent, Adult,* and *Child* when ego states are referred to, than to put them in quotation marks.)

It would be inexact to consider that these three entities are merely neologisms for the superego, ego, and id of Freud (1949). The superego is "a special agency within the ego" whose predominant function is a critical control, while the Parent is a complete ego state in itself. The patient whose (mother) Parent predominates habitually or at a given moment is not acting *as though* her mother "observes, orders, corrects, and threatens," (ibid.) but instead is acting *just like* her mother did, perhaps even with the same gestures and intonations. She is not acting with one eye on her mother, so to speak; she is reproducing her mother's total behavior, including her inhibitions, her reasoning, and (this is the crucial factor) her impulses. The decisive point is this: since her mother also had Parent, Adult, and Child components in her personality, the patient in the parental state is not merely critically prejudiced (mother's Parent), but also perceives reality the way her mother did, with the same distortions and emphases (mother's Adult), and furthermore, permits herself the same lapses from mature behavior that her mother did (mother's Child). This is shown in *Figure 5*, where the patient's Parent is subdivided into its own components. The P of the patient's Parent then represents grandmother, the A is mother's normally or abnormally distorted perceptions of reality, and the C comprises fixated archaic ego states of the mother.

In order to clarify this further, let us go back for a moment to distinguish between the patient who acts *like mother* and the one who acts *as mother would have liked.* The first has an active parental ego state; the second has an active child ego state: she behaves as she once behaved while mother was watching her, but she does not behave like mother.

Although there are theoretical differences which become significant in advanced work, for ordinary purposes

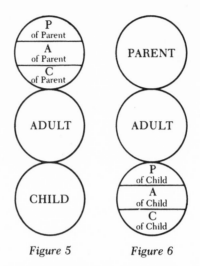

Figure 5   Figure 6

it is not necessary to distinguish between the Adult and Freud's "ego." Both have the task of dealing simultaneously with internal and external forces, and both are most clearly manifested when the individual is attempting to deal objectively with external reality.

The Child, archaic as it is, is still an organized ego state, while the id, according to Freud (1933), is "a chaos . . . it has no organization and no unified will." The organization of the Child is just as highly developed as it was when the individual was one, two, or three years old, or whenever the original fixating event occurred. It includes an archaic Parent, an archaic Adult, and a still more archaic Child representing a still earlier ego state to which under stress it may return. A simple illustration of the last is a three-year-old boy who reverts to previously abandoned thumb sucking when a baby brother is born. The Adult and the Parent in the actual child are exactly what Piaget (1932, 1954) is principally interested in: his construction of reality and his moral judgment. If the actual child's ego state, already endowed with all three components, becomes fixated through some untoward development in his emotional life, then after he grows up, this fixated ego state remains as the Child component in his personality, and can be revived in dreams, in hypnosis, in psychosis, in psychoanalysis, and sometimes even in memory or in everyday behavior. This situation is represented in *Figure 6.*

Thus superego-ego-id and Parent-Adult-Child are not synonymous or redundant, but represent different approaches. The present scheme is more useful in everyday practice because it is easier for patients to understand and easier for therapists to learn, aside from the question of its theoretical precision. An enlightening conceptual link between the two systems is provided by another point of view which has interesting neurological connotations. Both superego and Parent imply that "a portion of the external world has become an integral part of the internal world" (Freud, 1949). Hence both are in origin exteropsychic, and this aspect of the mind may be called the exteropsyche. Both the ego and the Adult develop partly autonomously through the organization of archaic potentialities into new faculties, such as logical thinking, which is both phylogenetically and ontogenetically a relatively late acquisition. This neoteric organization is called the neopsyche. By the same token both the id and the Child are archaic, and hence may be labelled archaeopsyche.

Some may prefer to use the terms *exteropsyche, neopsyche,* and *archaeopsyche* instead of *Parent, Adult,* and *Child,* but the terminology is not the main issue. The practical problem is how to distinguish these three components clinically, and how to go about using the distinction therapeutically in a manner that will be most easily understood by the patient. This system has been tested on a child, an adolescent, and a man with an IQ of 90, and by the use of carefully adapted wording, it became both intellectually and emotionally meaningful to all of them. The therapeutic effect is accounted for dynamically on the principle that psychic energy can shift or be attracted from one ego state to another, and that this shift is influenced by intrapsychic factors and by external relationships, both of which can be controlled with a certain degree of precision under favorable conditions.

Diagnostic Clarification

When it was suggested, on the basis of experience, that this approach was relatively easy to teach, this was not meant to imply that expertness could be attained by reading one introductory paper. The clinician who can devote some time to clarifying the boundaries between his own ego states has a decided advantage in dealing with patients. This form of self-analysis is much less subject to intrinsic difficulties than is the attempt at orthodox self-analysis.

Meanwhile, a familiar example may be offered to clarify further the diagnostic distinction between Parent, Adult, and Child. A young woman was referred by her family physician for a diagnostic interview because she was acting in a peculiar way that suggested psychosis. She was invited into the office and offered a chair. She sat tensely for a minute or two with downcast eyes and then began to laugh. After this, she looked stealthily at the doctor, averted her eyes from his gaze once more, and soon started to laugh again. This was repeated three or four times. Then rather suddenly she stopped tittering, sat up straight in her chair, pulled down her skirt, and turned her head to the right. The doctor observed this intent new attitude for a few minutes and then asked:

"Are you hearing voices?"

The patient nodded without turning her head, and continued to listen. After a few minutes of silence, the doctor asked gently but firmly what he judged to be a useful but innocuous question:

"How old are you?"

His tone successfully captured her attention. She stopped listening, turned her head to face him, and replied: "Twenty-five." Following this, she answered a series of other pertinent questions concisely and to the point, demonstrating that her understanding, her memory, and her ability to think logically were all intact. Within a short time, enough information was obtained to warrant a tentative diagnosis of acute schizophrenia, and to enable the doctor to piece together some of the precipitating factors and some of the gross features in the early background. After this, no further questions were put for awhile, whereupon she repeated the cycle: flirtatious tittering followed by listening, and then again facing the doctor to answer coherently a few more questions.

This time she was asked whose voices they were and what they were saying to her. She said that it seemed to be a man's voice and that he was calling her awful names, words she had never heard before. Then the talk was turned to her family. Her father was a wonderful man, and so forth. But sometimes he used to drink, and then he was different. He used bad language. In fact, come to think of it, he used some of the very epithets that the voices were using.

Here the three different ego states manifested themselves openly in cyclic fashion as tittering, scolding, and answering, respectively. She behaved differently and there was good reason to suppose from her facial expression and posture that she felt differently during each phase. There was a certain amount of flinging herself about during the tittering, so that this might be characterized as an archaic exhibitionistic method of seduction. This was terminated by pulling down her skirt as the voices, perceived as coming from outside herself, began to rebuke her. In the third state, she was able to answer questions like the grown-up woman that she was.

The special feature which made structural analysis easy in this case was the externalization of the Parent. When the sexual excitement of the Child reached a certain pitch, the Parent cut in sharply, whereupon the Child retreated and she pulled down her skirt. The Adult only came to the fore when outside reality, in the person of the doctor, intervened, whereupon both the scolding Parent and the tittering or contrite Child subsided. The test was provided when she related first, that she had never heard those words before, and later recalled that they were the very obscene words her father had used in his drunken rage.

The diagnosis of ego states is simple at times and lies in the following factors. The Parent is manifested in the language, intonations, normative attitude, and sometimes the posture and mannerisms of one or both of the patient's parents. The Adult is manifested in accomplishments which are beyond a child, such as accurate analysis of complex realities, and realistic manipulation of concepts. The Child is manifested in childlike behavior and attitudes and archaic modes of relationship and communication.

Sometimes the Child can be more clearly perceived by listening with closed eyes, so that the visual distraction of the physical adult is eliminated, whereupon certain vocal mannerisms and intonations become very suggestive, particularly to people accustomed to dealing with children. Under these conditions, the familiarity of certain intonations, such as plaintiveness, justification, wheedling, and so forth, is quite striking. The Parent may be similarly detected, particularly by those with pediatric experience, who may soon begin to recognize well-known types of mothers or fathers modulating the tones of their patients' voices.

Therapeutic Technique

The actual technique of structural analysis in the initial state is illustrated in the following case excerpt.

A 22-year-old woman was hospitalized in a severe state of agitation two months after the birth of her second child. After four weeks, the family physician requested her release for a trial of ambulatory treatment because she was badly needed at home. She was discharged with a diagnosis of schizophrenia, previously compensated by an obsessive-compulsive neurosis, now decompensated. The physician attempted to control her condition by large doses of chlorpromazine, up to 500 mg per day, but her emotional outbursts recurred with such severity that it appeared doubtful if she could continue outside the hospital.

The writer was called in consulation for psychotherapy, and was soon able to demonstrate to the patient that a considerable part of her personality (the Adult) was intact, and that the difficulties arose because a special state of mind (the Child) predominated. After two weeks, the chlorpromazine was discontinued, and she was put on a rigid regime of baths, exercises, triple bromides every three hours, and a detailed "going to bed" procedure with seconal. The expected frequent departures from this regime were ignored until the patient herself brought them to the fore through her clamorous complaints. This situation was used to illustrate the Child's way of handling reality, and also served indirectly to introduce the question of parental influences in her personality. For example, her dishonesty with the therapist was primarily motivated by the Child, but the Adult concurred, which illustrated the contamination of the Adult by the Child. But the Child must have had tacit permission from the Parent to permit herself such duplicity; hence it could be concluded that one or both of her actual parents must have been overtly dishonest during her early years. She was able to understand all this, and reluctantly described her father's policy of cheating in business, with mother's assistance, which she had been aware of in childhood; and indeed, gross dishonesty seemed to run through many of their relationships.

As her Adult objectivity toward both her Child and her Parent increased, it became possible to discontinue regular medication in the sixth week of treatment after 20 hours of psychotherapy, although she still took an occasional bromide when she was especially disturbed. The Adult now predominated throughout her interviews so that she could laugh, enjoy the discussion, and for the most part talk sensibly and judiciously. But as soon as the moment for parting arrived, the Child was once more overwhelmed with panic, the Adult was almost instantaneously decommissioned, and the therapist found himself dealing with the same agitated Child as before. The patient tried desperately to cling to the hour, using every excuse to prolong the interview, nagging the therapist coercively with doubts and questions. At an appropriate time, this "termination" behavior was examined in a typical session of structural analysis.

Her fear of dirt was first discussed. It was apparent that two systems were at work here, and that the neurotic anxiety resided in the Child. The Adult felt her obsessions and compulsions to be dystonic, and it was easy to establish a firm boundary between Adult and Child in this area, as in *Figure 1b*, which was drawn for the patient as a visual illustration of what had been accomplished. After this had been demonstrated to her satisfaction, the question of her nagging was broached. This was a contaminated area *(Figure 2a)* where she had no insight, since it was both Child and Adult syntonic. It was pointed out that her questions at the end of the hour were not "Adult" questions. She either knew the answers, knew that they were unanswerable, or knew that the answers lay outside the province of the therapist. One recurring question at this time, for example, was what to do about her maid leaving. It was apparent that this was a question for an employment agency rather than for a psychiatrist. In short, her questions were not based on a thoughtful quest for information, but on a need for something which was more characteristic of a very insecure child than of a curious adult. Yet at the moment she asked them, they evidently appeared appropriate to her. Now she could see that they were motivated by a need for reassurance or manipulation on the part of the Child rather than by a need for information on the part of the Adult.

The patient's response to this discussion was to express resentment against her mother for babying her. She gave examples of how she had begged her mother to do things for her that she could do well for herself. Her mother should not have given in. In other words, while the question about the maid was on the surface "adult," it was really an attempt at coercive seduction on the part of the Child. This clarified the difference between an Adult question and a Child question, so that her demands to know whether she was getting better, and whether she should not return to the hospital, now appeared to be ambivalent. The Adult wanted to hear that she was getting better, but the harrassed Child wanted to be sent to a hospital. Thus whichever way the therapist might have answered would have been "wrong." In fact, whenever anyone did answer such a question for her, she immediately went about demonstrating that the answer was unsatisfactory. At this point it was possible to illustrate the situation by drawing diagrams 2a and 2b.

After several of these demands had been analyzed in this way, two things were clear: first, the Adult was asking one question, but the Child wanted the answer to another, or wanted the opposite answer to the Adult. Secondly, that the questions were all connected with the Child's operation of "coercive nagging." The solution was not to reprimand the Child, or even to prohibit questions, but to find out what the Child was really trying to accomplish by this procedure and where and why she had learned it. The important effect of this discussion was to decontaminate the Adult. At the end of the session, "nagging" was still permissable and was still Child syntonic, but it was no longer Adult syntonic. The therapist now had a valuable ally in dealing with this problem. As the patient left, the Child took over for a brief moment as she started to ask a whining question once more. But she stopped in the middle, smiled merrily, and said: "There I go again!"

Results

Twenty-three prepsychotic, psychotic, and postpsychotic patients were treated by this method between September 1954 and September 1956. Without the writer's going into the difficult question of therapeutic criteria, let it be said that 18 of these (78%) steadfastly inproved by both subjective and objective standards, and three held their own. The remaining two were classified as therapeutic failures and were rehospitalized at their own suggestion; one because he was afraid he might lose control, the other because she could not sustain her lucid intervals in the face of external stress. Among 42 non-psychotic patients treated during this period the results were less apparent. Sixty-seven percent improved by the same criteria, and 33 percent merely held their own.

For various reasons it is not profitable to compare these results with earlier experiences of the therapist, before the present method was applied. It is possible, however, to offer figures that demonstrate the increased interest of patients in this method as compared with other approaches. During the years 1951-54, when the writer was using "psychoanalytic" group therapy, the gross attendance in various groups ranged from 83 to 89 percent. When he shifted experimentally to an "existential" approach for six months, the range dropped to 68-77 percent. During the year 1955, after the present approach had been adopted, the range was from 89 to 94 percent. Furthermore, during the "psychoanalytic" period, avoidable (resistance) absences were 9.4 percent of the total possible attendance; during the "existential" period they were 21.4 percent; and during the year 1955 they were only 7.4 percent. (The criteria for scoring attendance are discussed in detail elsewhere [Berne, 1955].)

Practical Suggestions

Experience has shown that the clinician who wishes to make a serious investigation of the possibilities of this kind of structural analysis in his own practice is well advised to overlook the Parent for the first six months or so, until he has acquired some facility in distinguishing between archaeopsychic and neopsychic manifestations. The results

from even this circumscribed application may be sufficiently gratifying to give him a real incentive to go
further. Similarly, the patient should have an opportunity
to become thoroughly familiar with his Child and his
Adult before he is introduced to his Parent. Exceptions to
this are certain resistant, compensated schizophrenics who
for defensive reasons have to repudiate strongly the
Child's activity and are unable to accord recognition to
this aspect; in such cases, the initial work should be
concerned with the boundary between the Parent and the
Adult, and discussion of the Child should be postponed.
In any case, interpretations should always follow at a
respectful distance behind clinical material.

As the therapist becomes familiar with all three aspects
of the patient, the probable reactions of each should be
weighed before each intervention, and none of them
should be slighted, deceived, or threatened. The
therapist should consider which aspect of his own personality motivates each intervention. His Parent may be
seduced or aroused by the patient's Child; his Child may
be dominated or annoyed by the patient's Parent. When
his Adult speaks, he should observe which aspect of the
patient is activated to respond.

The object of the treatment is to enable the Child to
make the fullest contribution to the patient's personality
with the Adult in the executive position. It does not
appear to be constructive to refer to archaeopsychic manifestations as childish; they may be more objectively
described as childlike, with reference to a child of a
certain conjectured age. The Child is preferably dealt
with according to the best pediatric principles, without
domination, derogation, or threat. Similarly, for seman-
tic reasons, the terms "mature" and "immature" should
be avoided as misleading. It is not so much that "the
patient is mature" or "the patient is immature"; rather, it

is a question of which ego state predominates in a given situation: Adult, Parent, or Child. For theoretical reasons, well supported by clinical experience, it may be safely assumed without sentimentality that in any patient who has once been a child, who has been subjected to parental influences, and who has had some measure of autonomous growth, any of the three aspects can be activated by appropriate measures. The Adult should be searched for, unmasked, and decontaminated.

Summary

1. A new psychotherapeutic approach is presented, based on the separation and reintegration of extero-psychic, neopsychic, and archaeopsychic influences in the patient's mind.

2. These three types of influences are subsumed under the terms *Parent, Adult,* and *Child,* respectively. Parent, Adult, and Child are distinguished from superego, ego, and id by the fact that the latter are "mental agencies" (Freud, 1949), while each of the former is a complete ego state in itself.

3. Psychiatric problems arise when the three ego states are in such severe conflict with each other that the Adult cannot maintain adequate control, or when he is pathologically contaminated by one or both of the others.

4. Structural analysis as a psychotherapeutic procedure consists of clarifying and strengthening the boundaries between the three ego states, and decontaminating the Adult. The purified, strengthened Adult is then in a better position to become the executive of a healthy way of living, and is a valuable ally in subsequent therapeutic work.

5. Cases are presented to illustrate the technique and

effects of structural analysis. The theoretical background is briefly outlined, practical suggestions are given, and the results in a series of cases are discussed. Of 65 patients treated by this method during the past two years, there were two therapeutic failures, 17 held their own, and 46 improved by both subjective and objective criteria.

7 Transactional Analysis: A New and Effective Method of Group Therapy

THERE IS NEED for a new approach to psychodynamic group therapy specifically designed for the situation it has to meet. The usual practice is to bring into the group methods borrowed from individual therapy, hoping, as occasionally happens, to elicit a specific therapeutic response. I should like to present a different system, one which has been well tested and is more adapted to its purpose, where group therapists can stand on their own ground rather than attempt a thinly spread imitation of the sister discipline.

Individual analytic therapy is characterized generally by the production of and a search for material, with interpersonal transactions holding a special place, typically in the field of "transference resistance" or "transference reactions." In a group, the systematic search for material is hampered because from the beginning the multitude of transactions takes the center of the stage. Therefore it seems appropriate to concentrate deliberately and specifically on analyzing such transactions. Structural analysis, and its later development into transactional analysis, in my experience, offers the most productive framework for this undertaking. Experiments with

Copyright, 1958, *The American Journal of Psychotherapy* (*12*, 735-743), by whom this reprint was permitted.

both approaches demonstrate certain advantages of structural and transactional analysis over attempts at psychoanalysis in the group. Among them are increased patient interest as shown by attendance records; increased degree of therapeutic success as shown by reduction of gross failures; increased stability of results as shown by long-term adjustment; and wider applicability in difficult patients such as psychopaths, the mentally retarded, and pre and postpsychotics. In addition, the intelligibility, precision, and goals of the therapeutic technique are more readily appreciated by the properly prepared therapist and patient alike.

This approach is based on the separation and investigation of exteropsychic, neopsychic, and archaeopsychic ego states. Structural analysis refers to the intrapsychic relationships of these three types of ego states: their mutual isolation, conflict, contamination, invasion, predominance, or cooperation within the personality. Transactional analysis refers to the diagnosis of which particular ego state is active in each individual during a given transaction or series of transactions, and of the understandings or misunderstandings which arise because of the perception or misperception of this factor by the individuals involved.

I have discussed in . . . [the last chapter] the nature of ego states in general, and of their classification according to whether they are exteropsychic (that is, borrowed from external sources); neopsychic (that is, oriented in accordance with current reality); or archaeopsychic (that is, relics fixated in childhood). These distinctions are easily understood by patients when they are demonstrated by clinical material, and when the three types are subsumed under the more personal terms *Parent, Adult,* and *Child,* respectively.

As this is a condensation in a very small space of a whole

146

psychotherapeutic system, I can only offer a few illustrative situations, choosing them for their relative clarity and dramatic quality in the hope that they will draw attention to some of the basic principles of structural and transactional analysis.

Structural Analysis

The first concerns a patient named Matthew, whose manner, posture, gestures, tone of voice, purpose, and field of interest varied in a fashion which at first seemed erratic. Careful and sustained observation, however, revealed that these variables were organized into a limited number of coherent patterns. When he was discussing his wife, he spoke in loud, deep, dogmatic tones, leaning back in his chair with a stern gaze and counting off the accusations against her on his upraised fingers. At other times he talked with another patient about carpentry problems in a matter-of-fact tone, leaning forward in a companionable way. On still other occasions, he taunted the other group members with a scornful smile about their apparent loyalty to the therapist, his head slightly bowed and his back ostentatiously turned to the leader. The other patients soon became aware of these shifts in his ego state, correctly diagnosed them as Parent, Adult, and Child, respectively, and began to look for appropriate clues concerning Matthew's actual parents and his childhood experiences. Soon everyone in the group, including the patient, was able to accept the simple diagram shown in *Figure 7* as a workable representation of Matthew's personality structure.

In the course of Matthew's therapy, he asked the physician to examine his father, who was on the verge of a paranoid psychosis. The therapist was astonished, in spite

MATTHEW
Structural Analysis

Figure 7

of his anticipations, to see how exactly Matthew's Parent reproduced the father's fixated paranoid ego state. During his interview, Matthew's father spoke in loud, deep, dogmatic tones, leaning back in his chair with a stern gaze, and counting off on his upraised fingers his accusations against the people around him.

. . . [Again,] Parent, Adult, and Child are not synonymous with superego, ego, and id. The latter are "psychic agencies," (Freud, 1949) while the former are complete ego states, each in itself including influences from superego, ego, and id. For example, when Matthew reproduced the Parental ego state, he not only behaved like a stern father, but also distorted reality the way his father did, and vented his sadistic impulses. And as cathexis was transferred from the Parental ego state into that of the scornful Child, the planning of his attacks and the accompanying guilt feelings had a childlike quality.

In therapy, the first task was to clarify in Matthew's

mind what was Parent, what was Adult, and what was Child in his feelings and behavior. The next phase was directed toward maintaining control through the Adult. The third phase was to analyze the current conflicts between the three ego states. Each of these phases brought its own kind of improvement, while the ultimate aim in this prepsychotic case was to enable all three ego states to cooperate in an integrated fashion as a result of structural analysis.

There were two contraindications in this case. The first was the universal indication against telling the Child to grow up. One does not tell a two-year-old to grow up. In fact, from the beginning it is necessary in every case to emphasize that we are not trying to get rid of the Child. The Child is not to be regarded as "childish" in the derogatory sense, but childlike, with many socially valuable attributes which must be freed so that they can make their contribution to the total personality when the confusion in this archaic area has been straightened out. The Child in the individual is potentially capable of contributing to his personality exactly what a happy actual child is capable of contributing to family life. The second contraindication, which is specific to this type of case, was against investigating the history and mechanism of his identification with his father, which was a special aspect of his parental ego state.

Simple Transactional Analysis

A patient named Camellia, following a previous train of thought, said that she had told her husband she wasn't going to have intercourse with him anymore and that he could go and find himself some other woman. Another patient named Rosita asked curiously "Why did you do that?" Whereupon Camellia, much to Rosita's discomfort, burst into tears and replied: "I try so hard, and then you criticize me."

This transaction may be analyzed according to the diagram in *Figure 8*. This figure was drawn and analyzed for the group as follows. The personalities of the two women are represented structurally as comprising Parent, Adult, and Child. The original *transactional stimulus* is Camellia's statement about what she told her husband. She related this in her Adult ego state, with which the group was familiar. It was received in turn by an Adult Rosita, who in her response exhibited a mature, reasonable interest in the story. As shown in *Figure 8a*, the transactional stimulus was Adult to Adult and so was the transactional response. If things had continued at this level, the conversation might have proceeded smoothly.

Rosita's question ("Why did you do that?") now constituted a new transactional stimulus, and was intended as

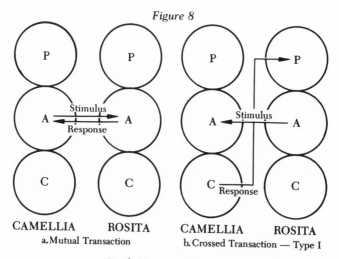

Figure 8

CAMELLIA ROSITA
a. Mutual Transaction

CAMELLIA ROSITA
b. Crossed Transaction — Type I

Simple Transactional Analysis

Figure 9

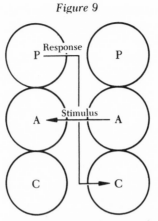

MATTHEW Another Member
Crossed Transaction — Type II

one adult speaking to another. Camellia's weeping response, however, was not that of one adult to another, but that of a child to a critical parent. Camellia's misperception of Rosita's ego state, and the shift of her own ego state, resulted in a crossed transaction and broke up the conversation which now had to take another turn. This is represented in *Figure 8b.*

This particular type of crossed transaction, in which the stimulus is Adult to Adult, and the response is Child to Parent, is probably the most frequent cause of misunderstandings in marriage and work situations, as well as in social life. Clinically, it is typified by the classical transference reaction, which is a special case of the crossed transaction. In fact this particular species of crossed transaction may be said to be the chief problem of psychoanalytic technique.

In Matthew's case, when he was talking about his wife, the crossing was reversed. If one of the other members, as an Adult, asked him a question, expecting an Adult response, Matthew instead usually answered like a supercilious parent talking to a backward child, as represented in *Figure 9*.

Therapeutically, this simple type of transactional analysis helped Camellia to become more objective about her Child. As the Adult gained control, and the Child's responses at home were suppressed for later discussion in the group, her marital and social life improved even before any of the Child's confusion was resolved.

The Analysis of Games

Short sets of ongoing transactions may be called operations. These constitute tactical maneuvers, in which it is the other members of the group who are maneuvered. Thus the conversation between Camellia and Rosita, taken as a whole, is an operation, and has to be analyzed again at a deeper level, when it soon appears that the need of Camellia's Child to feel criticized was one of the motives for telling this particular story to the group.

A series of operations constitutes a "game." A game may be defined as a recurring series of transactions, often repetitive, superficially rational, with a concealed motivation or more colloquially, a series of operations with a "gimmick."

Hyacinth recounted her disappointment and resentment because a friend of hers had given a birthday party which she herself had planned to give. Camellia asked: "Why don't you give another party later?" To which Hyacinth responded: "Yes, but then it wouldn't be a birthday party." The other members of the group then began to give wise suggestions, each beginning with "Why don't you . . ." and to each of these Hyacinth gave a response which began: "Yes, but . . ."

Hyacinth had told her story for the purpose of setting in motion the commonest of all the games which can be observed in groups: the game of "Why don't you . . . Yes but . . ." This is a game which can be played by any number. One player, who is "it," presents a problem. The others start to present solutions, to each of which the one who is "it" objects. A good player can stand off the rest of the group for a long period, until they all give up, whereupon "it" wins. Hyacinth, for example, successfully objected to more than a dozen solutions before the therapist broke up the game. The gimmick in "Why don't you . . . Yes but . . ." is that it is played not for its ostensible purpose (a quest for information or solutions), but for the sake of the fencing; and as a group phenomenon it corresponds to Bion's basic assumption "F" (1952).

Other common games are "How Am I Doing?" "Uproar," "Alcoholic," "P.T.A.," "Ain't it Awful?" and "Schlemiel." In "Schlemiel," the one who is "it" breaks things, spills things, and makes messes of various kinds, and each time says: "I'm sorry!" This leaves the inexperienced player in a helpless position. The skillful opponent, however, says: "You can break things and spill things all you like; but please don't say 'I'm sorry!' " This response usually causes the Schlemiel to collapse or explode, since it knocks out his gimmick, and the opponent wins. I imagine that at this point many of you are thinking of Stephen Potter, but I think the games I have in mind are more serious; and some of them, like "Alcoholic," with all its complex rules published by various rescue organizations, are played for keeps. "Alcoholic" is complicated because the official form requires at least four players: a persecutor, a rescuer, a dummy, and the one who is "it."

The transactional analysis of Hyacinth's game of "Why don't you . . . Yes but . . ." is represented in *Figure 10.*

This figure was drawn and analyzed for the group. In the guise of an Adult seeking information, Hyacinth "cons" the other members into responding like sage parents advising a helpless child. The object of Hyacinth's Child is to confound these parents one after the other. The game can proceed because at the superficial level, both stimulus and response are Adult to Adult, and at a deeper level they are also complementary, Parent to Child stimulus ("Why don't you . . .?") eliciting Child to Parent response ("Yes, but . . ."). The second level is unconscious on both sides.

The therapeutic effect of this analysis was to make Hyacinth aware of her defensive need to confound, and to make the others aware of how easily they could be conned into taking a parental role unawares. When a new patient tried to start a game of "Why don't you . . . Yes but . . ." in this group, they all played along with her in order not

Figure 10

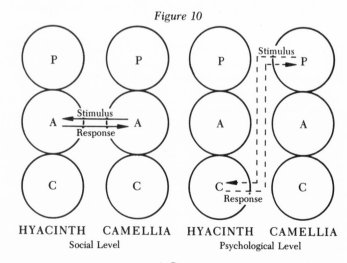

| HYACINTH | CAMELLIA | HYACINTH | CAMELLIA |
| Social Level | | Psychological Level | |

A Game

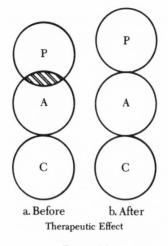

a. Before   b. After

Therapeutic Effect

Figure 11

to make her too anxious, but after a few weeks they gently demonstrated to her what was happening. In other words, they now had the option of playing or not playing this game, as they saw fit, where formerly they had no choice but to be drawn in. This option was the net therapeutic gain, which they were able to apply profitably in their more intimate relationships. In structural terms, this improvement is presented in *Figure 11*. *Figure 11a* shows the original contamination of the Adult by the Parent and *Figure 11b* shows the decontaminated Adult which can now rationally control their behavior in this particular situation.

The Analysis of Scripts

A script is an attempt to repeat in derivative form not a transference reaction or a transference situation, but a transference drama, often split into acts, exactly like the theatrical scripts which are intuitive artistic derivatives of these primal dramas of childhood. Operationally, a script is a complex set of transactions, by nature recurrent, but not necessarily recurring, since a complete performance may require a whole lifetime. A common tragic script is that based on the rescue fantasy of a woman who marries one alcoholic after another. The disruption of such a script leads to despair Since the magical cure of the alcoholic husband which the script calls for is not forthcoming, a divorce results and the woman tries again. A practical and constructive script, on the other hand, may lead to great happiness if the others in the cast are well chosen and play their parts satisfactorily. A game usually represents a segment of a script.

The ultimate goal of transactional analysis is the analysis of scripts, since the script determines the destiny and identity of the individual. Space, however, does not permit a discussion of the technique, aim, and therapeutic effect of script analysis, and this topic will have to be reserved for another communication.

Self-Analysis

Structural and transactional analysis lend themselves to self-examination more readily than orthodox psychoanalysis does since they effectively bypass many of the difficulties inherent in self-psychoanalysis. The therapist who has some knowledge of his own personality structure has a distinct advantage in dealing with his countertransference problems; that is, the activity of his own Child or Parent with its own favorite games, its own script, and its own motives for becoming a group therapist. If he has a clear insight, without self-delusion, as to what is exteropsychic, what is neopsychic, and what is archaeopsychic in himself, then he can choose his responses so as to bring the maximum therapeutic benefit to his patients.

I have condensed into this brief communication material which would easily fill a book, and which is best made clear by six months or a year of clinical supervision. In its present form, however, it might stimulate some people to more careful observation of ego states in their patients, and to some serious and sustained experiments in structural interpretation.

Summary

1. A new approach to group therapy is outlined, based on the distinction between exteropsychic, neopsychic, and archaeopsychic ego states. The study of relationships within the individual of these three types of ego states, colloquially called Parent, Adult, and Child, respectively, is termed structural analysis . . .

2. Once each individual in the group has some understanding of his own personality in these terms, the group can proceed to simple transactional analysis, in which the ego state of the individual who gives the transactional stimulus is compared with the ego state of the one who gives the transactional response.

3. In the next phase, short series of transactions, called operations, are studied in the group. More complex series may constitute a "game," in which some element of double-dealing or insincerity is present. In the final phase, it is demonstrated that all transactions are influenced by complex attempts on the part of each member to

manipulate the group in accordance with certain basic fantasies derived from early experiences. This unconscious plan, which is a strong determinant of the individual's destiny, is called a script.

4. Clinical examples are given, and the therapeutic gain expected from each phase of structural and transactional analysis is indicated.

8 *The Psychodynamics of Intuition*

I N . . . [THE PRECEDING chapters] various aspects of clinical intuition were discussed: intuition of social factors such as occupation, diagnostic intuition, the problem of latent communications, intuitions concerning instinctual strivings, and intuitions concerning the patient's ego state. The ultimate question of how intuition can be cultivated, controlled, and activated at will still remains unanswered, and for some decades or even centuries may stay in the province of metaphysical speculation. Meanwhile, clinical observation does provide some hints, at least as to the conditions under which this faculty is most likely to function effectively. Some of the external conditions were outlined in the first paper of this series. The present communication will deal with the psychodynamics of intuition; that is, with the internal conditions which promote or interfere with the workings of the intuitive process.

The term "intuitive individual" as used here is not intended to refer to the "intuitive type" of Jungian psychology, but to the clinician who deliberately uses his intuitive faculties when desirable in his diagnostic and

Copyright 1962, *The Psychiatric Quarterly* (36, 294-300), by whom this reprint was permitted. (Originally entitled, "Intuition VI: The Psychodynamics of Intuition.")

therapeutic work. Descriptively, such a clinician is curious, mentally alert, interested, and receptive of latent and manifest communications from his patients. Genetically, these attitudes are well-sublimated derivatives of scopophilia, watchfulness, and oral receptivity. Secondary gains may be influential in activating this state of mind in laymen: attention in the socially insecure, financial profit in confidence men, and power hunger in leaders of men and seducers of women. These gains are related to genital exhibitionism, anal trickery, and oral sadism, respectively. Thus intuitions may be used as instruments for satisfaction at any level of psychosexual development. This refers only to intuitions proper; that is, intuitions about people, and not to hunches about events. Perhaps the commonest example is the ability of homosexuals to spot one another quickly. . . .

The clinician who is afraid of his own scopophilia, his need to be alert, or his own oral receptivity, is also likely to repress or suppress his own intuitive faculties, or even to criticize or scoff at others who are more at ease with them. Conversely, if the individual abuses his intuition for the sake of the secondary gains, if he is too anxious for attention, profit, or power, it may fail him. If he is too eager to be exhibitionistic, tricky, or sadistic, he will overexploit himself and in effect sterilize the goose that lays the golden egg. Between these two extremes, the intuitive individual, to be consistently successful, must be a well-balanced person. Curiously enough, however, a feeling of omnipotence or omniscience does not seem to interfere with the exercise of intuition, although it may cause interpersonal difficulties and is better curbed.

There is little doubt that intuition is an archaic faculty. It is well known that "logical" thinking interferes with its efficiency and distorts its messages. Ferenczi once remarked that education is not only the acquisition of new faculties but is also the forgetting of others, which, if not forgotten, would be called "supernormal." Intuition does not seem to be "supernormal," but it is certainly something which modern education does not tend to encourage. Engineers and psychologists are among the most highly educated individuals in modern society and at the same time have, generally speaking, the greatest resistance against intuitive cognition. The psychologist who wishes to engage in clinical work is forced to resurrect this lost faculty if he is to be successful, and for that very reason he is often derogated by his more academic colleagues. It is not so well known that "ethical" thinking also interferes with intuition, a point which will be illustrated shortly.

Although intuition has the quality of an archaic process, revealing its insights most readily when neopsychic faculties are at rest, as in the hypnogogic state, it cannot be called a manifestation of the id, since, according to Freud, the id is merely "a chaos, a cauldron of seething excitement," with no organization (1933, p. 104) and no direct relations with the external world (1949, p. 108). In Freudian structural terminology, it is most conveniently classed as a faculty of the archaic ego. It is more readily understood, however, in a slightly different structural framework in which psychic influences are considered, not in the classical conceptual triad of id, ego, and superego, but from a functional point of view as archaeopsychic, neopsychic, or exteropsychic in origin. These three types of influences manifest themselves phenomenologically as archaeopsychic, neopsychic, or exteropsychic ego states, which may be colloquially spoken of as Child, Adult, and Parent ego states, respectively. . . .

In this terminology, it can be said that intuition is an archaeopsychic phenomenon. Hence its function is repressed when the neopsychic Adult ego state predominates, and is impaired when the exteropsychic Parent ego state encroaches on the freedom of the archaeopsyche.

161

Operationally, this means that both logical thinking and "ethical" thinking impair the efficiency of intuition. The latter point will now be illustrated by an example.

The writer once told some friends that he had gone to a café and played chess with a man who was sitting there before a chessboard drinking coffee, that the man was a waiter, and that, as a professional intellectual, the writer was somewhat chagrined at being beaten at chess by a waiter.

"You mean that he was a waiter in the café?" asked the friends.

"No, no. He was a customer, and he was just sitting there enjoying his coffee."

"How did you know he was a waiter? Was he dressed like a waiter?"

"No, he was dressed like anybody else, but you could tell he was a waiter."

"How could you tell?"

"Because you can tell when a man is a waiter just as you can tell when a man is a plainclothes policeman, after you've met one. A waiter looks like a waiter, and a plainclothesman looks like a plainclothesman. Any competent criminal can spot a plainclothes policeman, no matter what kind of clothes he's wearing. And vice versa, for that matter."

"It just sounds snobbish to me," said one of the friends.

"Me too," said another, "I couldn't tell a waiter on sight. Waiters are just people like you and me. They're not some special kind of animal."

"They're not a special kind of animal," replied the writer, "but they are a special kind of man."

It should be added, if it is not already clear, that the

friends were Democrats, which is the essential point of this story. A real Democrat is supposed to regard all people as equal members of the human race, and it is a kind of wickedness to distinguish them by trade. This is an example of "ethical" thinking, imposed from without by parents or people who are *in loco parentis,* and reinforced continually by other people who are *in loco parentis* as far as education is concerned. Hence the attitude that it is snobbish, and thus in Democratic dialect unethical, to distinguish people socially by trade, is of exteropsychic origin, and constitutes an intrusion of the Parent ego state on the freedom of the archaeopsyche. The friends in question were in truth quite unperceptive regarding occupational identity, and their disapproval of such perceptions interfered with their intuition in this respect. This is analogous to a certain kind of countertransference problem at the clinical level, where a therapist's prejudice (in favor of creative personalities, or against wife beaters, for example) keeps him from perceiving his patient clearly. Both situations demonstrate that parental influences can impair the archaeopsychic intuitive capacity as effectively as neopsychic "logical" thinking can.

Structurally, then, intuition is an archaeopsychic faculty. Dynamically, its efficiency can be impaired by neopsychic or exteropsychic activity. Hence it works best when an archaeopsychic ego state predominates, and when neopsychic and exteropsychic ego states are decathected and decommissioned. This conclusion is confirmed by the observations noted in the first paper of this series. Similarly, fears of one's own scopophilia, one's need to be alert, or oral receptivity, which seem to hinder the intuitive process, are based on exteropsychic influences, so that again it is those influences which cause difficulty by interfering with archaeopsychic freedom. There are some possible indications that, fundamentally, clinical intuition is a well-sublimated derivative of infantile cannibalistic tendencies, so that resistance to intuition may represent a failure of sublimation in this area.

In order to understand certain specific problems concerning intuition, it is necessary to consider the relationships between the three types of ego states, as they have been demonstrated in more detail elsewhere (Berne, 1961). In general, the younger the individual, the freer his archaeopsyche is from exteropsychic and neopsychic influences. Hence young children, in the manner hinted at by Ferenczi, can assess the potentialities of other people without interference from artifacts introduced by "education," which includes such factors as parental influences (exteropsychic) and logical thinking (neopsychic).

The truth of the matter is that people in all societies are taught not to look at each other except in the manner permitted by social sanctions. The infant, on the other hand, does not hesitate to stare at whichever part of the other person's body interests him the most. In addition, his libido is free to make whatever use he cares to of the data he gathers in this manner. Schizophrenics enjoy similar freedoms. Hence children and schizophrenics can gather more data and process this information in a more personal way than normal adults are permitted to do. In effect this means that their intuitive powers which are libidinally motivated, are less trammeled and more available to them, resulting in the often remarked "intuitiveness" of these two classes of people.

As a corollary, the more "ethical" a person is, the more mannerly and philanthropic in deed and thought, the less his powers of observation and intuition are free to function without unconscious moral intervention. The effect is similar if his observations and appraisals are narrowed to meet the demands of logical categories. If his logic or ethics are in the nature of reaction formations, his powers of observation will be still further stultified, and in addition, productions from the archaeopsyche will be subject to more active moral or intellectual distortion. Both the constriction and the distortion will contribute to erroneous judgments. Even if he starts off with a correct, if stilted, assessment, it will be warped for defensive reasons into something different. Confusion in the archaeopsyche itself may have a similar effect. A man who appears "bad" to a child of a certain age can sometimes make himself appear "good" by a direct appeal to the child's oral needs, such as an offer of candy, which fogs, temporarily at least, the first intuitive impression. This kind of approach is well known to confidence men and other exploiters. After the fogging clears, the original impression may emerge clearly again.

For the intuitive clinician, the whole mechanism must be sublimated, that is, delibidinized and put in the service of his neopsyche and his exteropsyche's social aims. To make his intuitive capacities available in his work, he must have a clear separation between the three types of ego states. His archaeopsyche must be able to function independently during a longer or shorter period of observation; he must be free to observe and to integrate his data as an infant would, without interference from morals or logic. The impressions thus gained must be delivered to the neopsyche so that they can be translated into clinical language, and exploited under the influence of the exteropsyche for the benefit of the patient. The effect is that of a kind of psychological robbery to which the libidinous archaeopsyche becomes a willing victim, perhaps in return for other gains such as a feeling of omniscience. If this feeling becomes too greatly desired, further accretions may be sought by the delivery of adul-

165

terated or *ersatz* goods—a further source of inaccurate intuitions. Hence, as soon as the clinician becomes over-confident about his intuition, it is time for a rest. On the other hand, if the sublimation is incomplete, the archaeopsyche may try to exploit its intuitions for its own pleasure; in that case, greed, overeagerness, or anxiety may lead to incomplete or distorted assessments.

In this system, the intellect enters as follows: What are "conclusions" for the archaeopsyche become "data to be processed" for the neopsyche. The raw, unverbalized, but operative, intuitions regarding another person's instinctual tendencies are independent of the intellect, as demonstrated by the intuitive reactions of very young children; but the verbalization and sorting into logical frameworks of these raw intuitions are neopsyche functions, the efficiency of which will depend to some extent on the intellectual capacity of the individual.

Summary

The psychodynamics of intuition are considered from the viewpoints of psychoanalysis and "structural analysis." An example is offered to illustrate the fact that "ethical" as well as logical thinking can interfere with the intuitive process. Defenses against scopophilia, the need to be alert, and oral receptivity seem to give rise to a resistance against the whole topic. Conversely, intuitive faculties are porbably most readily available to individuals who have successfully sublimated scopophiliac, paranoid, and oral receptive tendencies. Sources of error, and the role of the intellect in clinical intuition, are discussed.

Bibliography

Ashby, W. R. A new mechanism which shows simple conditioning. *Journal of Psychology*, 1950, *29*, 343-347.

Bateson, G., & Ruesch, J. *Communication*. New York: Norton, 1951.

Bergler, E. The gambler. *Journal of Criminal Psychopathology*, 1943, *4*, 379-393.

Bergler, E. *The basic neurosis*. New York: Grune & Stratton, 1949.

Bergson, H. *Creative evolution*. New York: Modern Library, 1944.

Berkeley, E. C. *Giant brains*. New York: Wiley, 1949.

Berne, E. *The mind in action*. New York: Simon & Schuster, 1947.

Berne, E. Group attendance: Clinical and theoretical considerations. *International Journal of Group Psychotherapy*, 1955, *5*, 392-403.

Berne, E. *Transactional analysis in psychotherapy*. New York: Grove, 1961.

Bernfeld, S., & Feitelberg, S. Bericht über einige psychophysiologische Arbeiten. *Imago, Lpz.*, 1934, *20*, 224-231.

Bion, W. R. Group dynamics: A re-view. *International Journal of Psycho-Analysis*, 1952, *33*, 235-247.

Brillouin, L. Life, thermodynamics and cybernetics. *American Scientist*, 1949, *37*, 554-568.

Bibliography

Brillouin, L. Thermodynamics and information theory. *American Scientist*, 1950, *38*, 594-599.

Cohen, M. R. & Nagel, E. *An introduction to logic and scientific method.* New York: Harcourt, Brace, 1934.

Darwin, C. *Expression of the emotions in man and animals.* New York: Appleton, 1886.

Deutsch, H. *Psychology of women* (Vol. 1). New York: Grune & Stratton, 1944.

Eisenbud, J. Telepathy and problems of psychoanalysis. *Psychoanalytic Quarterly*, 1946, *15*, 32-87.

Erikson, E. H. *Childhood and society.* New York: Norton, 1950.

Federn, P. The undirected function in the central nervous system. *International Journal of Psychoanalysis*, 1938, *19*(2), 1-26.

Federn, P. *Ego psychology and the psychoses.* New York: Basic Books, 1952.

Fenichel, O. *The psychoanalytic theory of neurosis.* New York: Norton, 1945.

Ferenczi, S. *Sex in psycho-analysis.* Boston: Badger, 1916.

Freud, S. *New introductory lectures on psycho-analysis.* New York: Norton, 1933.

Freud, S. *Group psychology.* London: Hogarth, 1940.

Freud, S. *An outline of psychoanalysis.* New York: Norton, 1949.

Freud, S., & Breuer, J. *Studies in hysteria.* New York: Nervous and Mental Disease Publishing Co., 1937.

Fromm-Reichmann, F. Development of treatment of schizophrenics by psychoanalytic psychotherapy. *Psychiatry*, 1948, *11*, 263-273.

Gitelson, M. The emotional position of the analyst in the psychoanalytic situation. *International Journal of Psychoanalysis*, 1952, *33*, 1-10.

Hinsie, L. E., & Shatzky, J. *Psychiatric dictionary.* New

York: Oxford University Press, 1945. (See "perception, subconscious")

Hunt, J. McV. (Ed.). *Personality and the behavior disorders.* New York: Ronald, 1944.

Hutchinson, E. D. Varieties of insight in humans. *Psychiatry,* 1939, *2,* 323-332.

Jaensch, E. R. *Eidetic imagery.* London: Kegan Paul, 1930. (The writer has not had access to this work and has studied only extracts and summaries.)

Jones, E. The theory of symbolism. In *Papers on psychoanalysis.* New York: William Wood, 1923.

Jung, C. G. *Psychological types.* New York: Harcourt, Brace, 1946.

Kahn, E. *Psychopathic personalities.* New Haven: Yale University Press, 1931.

Kempf, E. J. *The autonomic functions and the personality.* New York: Nervous and Mental Disease Publishing Co., 1921.

Kestenberg, J. S. Notes on ego development. *International Journal of Psychoanalysis,* 1953, *34,* 111-122.

Kohler, W. *Gestalt psychology.* New York: Liveright, 1929.

Kris, E. On inspiration. *International Journal of Psychoanalysis,* 1939, *20,* 377-390.

Krogh, A. The language of the bees. *Scientific American,* August 1948, 18-21.

Kulp, J. L., Feely, H. W., & Tryon, L. E. Lamont natural radiocarbon measurements, I. *Science,* 1951, *114,* 565-568.

Maurer, D. W. *The big con.* New York: Pocket Books, 1949.

Mygatt, G. *Pageant,* September 1947.

Newman, J. R. The Rhind Papyrus. *Scientific American,* August 1952, *187,* 24-27.

Bibliography

Ostow, M. Entropy changes in mental activity. *Journal of Nervous and Mental Diseases,* 1949, *110,* 502-506.

Pederson-Krag, G. Telepathy and repression. *Psychoanalytic Quarterly,* 1947, *16,* 61-68.

Pei, M. *The story of language.* Philadelphia: Lippincott, 1949.

Penrose, L. S. Freud's theory of instinct and other psychobiological theories. *International Journal of Psychoanalysis,* 1931, *12,* 87-97.

Piaget, J. *The moral judgment of the child.* New York: Harcourt, Brace, 1932.

Piaget, J. *The construction of reality in the child.* New York: Basic Books, 1954.

Poincaré, H. Mathematical creation. (J. R. Newman, Ed.) *Scientific American,* August 1948, *179,* 54-57.

Rapaport, D. (Ed.). *Organization and pathology of thought.* New York: Columbia University Press, 1951.

Rashevsky, N. *Mathematical biophysics.* Chicago: University of Chicago Press, 1938.

Reik, T. *Listening with the third ear.* New York: Farrar, Straus, 1948.

Rhine, J. B. *New frontiers of the mind.* New York: Farrar & Rhinehart, 1937.

Ronchese, F. Calluses, cicatrices and other stigmata as an aid to personal identification. *Journal of American Medical Association,* 1945, *128,* 925-931.

Rosen, J. N. Treatment of schizophrenic psychosis by direct analytic therapy. *Psychiatric Quarterly,* 1947, *21,* 3-37; 117-119.

Schilder, P. *Mind.* New York: Columbia University Press, 1942.

Shannon, C. E. A chess-playing machine. *Scientific American,* February 1950, *182,* 48-51.

Shannon, C., & Weaver, W. *The mathematical theory of*

communication. Urbana: University of Illinois Press, 1949.

Sharpe, E. Psycho-physical problems revealed in language. In *Collected papers on psycho-analysis*. London: Hogarth, 1950.

Shatzky, J., & Hinsie, L. E. *Psychiatric dictionary*. New York: Oxford, 1940.

Silberer, H. In D. Rapaport, 1951, q.v.

Smythies, J. R. The "base line" of schizophrenia. *American Journal of Psychiatry*, 1953, *110*, 200-204.

Spitz, R. (Films shown at scientific meetings)

Stone, L. On the principal obscene word of the English language. *International Journal of Psychoanalysis*, 1954, *35*, 30-56.

Sturtevant, E. H. *An introduction to linguistic science*. New Haven: Yale University Press, 1947.

Symposium. Teleological mechanisms. *Annals of the New York Academy of Science*, 1948, *50*, 187-278.

Walter, W. G. An imitation of life. *Scientific American*, May 1950, *182*, 42-45.

Walter, W. G. A machine that learns. *Scientific American*, August 1951, *185*, 60-63.

Weiss, E. *Psychodynamics*. New York: Grune & Stratton, 1950.

Wiener, N. *Cybernetics, or control and communication in animal and machine*. New York: Wiley, 1948. (a)

Wiener, N. Time, communication, and the nervous system. *Annals of the New York Academy of Science*, 1948, *50*, 217. (b)

Wild, K. W. *Intuition*. London: Cambridge University Press, 1938.

Wittels, F. Review of Stekel's *Interpretation of dreams*. *Psychoanalytic Quarterly*, 1945, *19*, 542.

Index

Index

Index

A Note on the Editor

PAUL McCORMICK, the editor of TA Press and of this book, is a Clinical Teaching Member of the International Transactional Analysis Association. He took his introductory course in transactional analysis from Eric Berne, MD, in 1961, and has since been a student and practitioner of the method.

He attended Dr. Berne's weekly San Francisco Social Psychiatry Seminars from 1961 to 1965, and undertook additional supervision and training in TA with the Gouldings (Robert L., MD, and Mary, MSW) at the Western Institute for Group and Family Therapy.

He is the author of *Guide for Use of a Life Script Questionnaire,* and *Ego States: Parent, Adult, Child;* and coauthor, with Leonard Campos, PhD, of *Introduce Yourself to TA,* and *Introduce Your Marriage to TA* (all from Transactional Publications, distributor for TA Press and the ITAA).